VIRGILIO Card. NOE'

*the* # HOLY DOOR

*in* **ST. PETER**

ATS Italia Editrice
Libreria Editrice Vaticana

PAVLVS V PONT MAX ANNO XIIII

IOANNES PAVLVS II P.M.
PORTAM SANCTAM
ANNO IVBILAEI MCMLXXV
A PAVLO PP. VI
RESERATAM ET CLAVSAM
APERVIT ET CLAVSIT
ANNO IVB. HVMANAE REDEMP.
MCMLXXXIII - MCMLXXXIV

PAVLVS VI PONT MAX
HVIVS PATRIARCALIS
VATICANAE BASILICAE
PORTAM SANCTAM
APERVIT ET CLAVSIT
ANNO IVBILAEI MCMLXXV

# The Holy Door Tells its Story

*T*he beginning of the Holy Year is marked by opening a door called the Holy Door. It is the most important door offering access to the Basilica. The opening takes place during a specific ceremony at the beginning of the Holy Year or Jubilee. This is what happens on that occasion in the entrance of the church. After kneeling on the threshold, the Pope knocks on the door three times, reciting a prayer which clearly expresses the meaning of this gesture and of the events that will occur during the Jubilee: "O Lord, grant that the auspicious moment when this door is opened to all believers be a joyous one for Your church, as the faithful come inside and lift their prayers to You, receiving forgiveness, indulgence and the complete remission of their sins...." This prayer tells us what crossing the threshold of this door should mean to everyone who wants to take that step. It is an outward sign of inner renewal, which includes coming to terms with God, becoming reconciled with our fellow man, and amending the past, so that life can begin again according to God's rules.

*S*t.Peter's Holy Door has its own story to tell. Before this one, there was a Holy Door made of wood, which was inaugurated by Benedict XIV in 1748 and remained in place until the end of World War II.

Then the Bishop of Basil-Lugano, Mons. Francesco von Streng, gave Pius XII a new bronze Holy Door as a sign of the Swiss people's gratitude for having been spared the horrors of war. Pius XII blessed the door in a solemn inaugural ceremony for the Jubilee, and explained its iconography: "the bronze panels...movingly praise the wonders of mercy practised by God, who came to look for what had been lost."

During the next Jubilee, in the year 2000, a pope will kneel on this threshold for the fourth time since 1949, when Pius XII started a great process of renewal and forgiveness. Twenty-five years later, in 1975, Paul VI said that he hoped that the Jubilee would bring a renewal within both the Church and individuals, along the lines of Vatican II. In 1983 Pope John Paul II inaugurated a Jubilee year to remember the benefits of redemption, which fifty years previously had been celebrated the extraordinary Holy Year for Redemption ordered by Pius XI. In 1983, John Paul II said: "The Holy Door must be the sign and symbol of a new closeness to Christ, who is man's saviour". On Christmas night of 1999, John Paul II will lead the faithful into the new millennium, the third since the Incarnation took place.

Thinking about the four times that the Holy Door has been opened during the past half century, a question springs to mind: how many pilgrims passed through it during those occasions? The sum boggles human calculation! Only God knows what wonders have been accomplished, when human hearts opened to his grace, and the old saying "mercy is abundant with God" should also come true in the future.

# The Doors of the Bible

*T*he whole history of salvation in the Bible lies between two doors: the gate to Heaven, from which the first man was cast out after original sin, and the gate to the heavenly Jerusalem, through which one enters eternal salvation. However, the Bible mentions many other doors, almost as a reminder of their significance: the door of Jerusalem, made of sapphires and emeralds; the doors of the temple, which open up majestically towards the cardinal points. In the Gospels, an entire city gathers with all its sick people in front of Peter's house in Capernaum, while Jesus meets a funeral procession near the gates of the city of Naim, bringing back to life the only son of a poor widow.

The opening of some doors imparts a message. The door of one's room should be closed to recite prayers known only to our Heavenly Father. Even at nightime a door may open to the insistent pleading of a friend, begging for some bread. Christ's followers must all pass through a narrow door. Lazarus begs in front of the door of a rich man, who dresses in purple and fine linen and eats lavishly every day. The door of a marriage feast closes in front of five foolish and thoughtless girls, because they arrive

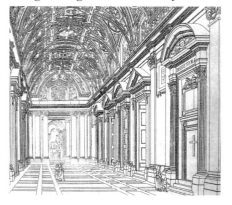

late and are not ready. Doors have many meanings in the Gospels, but one aspect of them must always be respected. They must never be crossed hurriedly; one should pause in front of each door, receiving its message or meditating on the Gospels.

*T*hese references to doors in the books of revelation tend to fade somewhat in the face of Christ's statement: "I am the door of the sheep". Having just said that he was the shepherd, who loved and knew his flock, Jesus stressed this concept, explaining: "I am the door: anyone passing through me will be saved, they will enter and exit and find pasture...". Life is given, in abundance. To enter this life, one must be fit for it: the door is narrow, and therefore one must be brought down to size by conversion. Jesus is shown knocking at everyone's door: "If one of you hears me calling and opens the door, I will come in and share a meal at that person's side". Christ, begging for love, wants to enter the innermost sphere of every man, woman and child. We are called to his Eucaristic banquet, where all God's children are united, but Christ also wants his disciples to feel his friendship: "Everyone who eats with me, will live for me." Anyone who opens the door to Christ is blessed. During the Middle Ages, mystics such as Bonaventure, Matilda and Gertrude shared a particular experience. They saw the image of Christ/Door in the heart of Christ, pierced on the cross by a spear. The wound in Christ's side, with water and blood flowing from it, is the door seen by Ezekiel on the right side of the temple, through which water gushed, and carried everyone away.

# The Church is the Door

*I*n the liturgy, the door of a church has always been seen as the passage used by mankind to approach God through Christ, listen to the Word, celebrate the Eucharist, pray, and generally contribute to the growth of God's people. Inscriptions on doors often contained references to this role:

IANVA SVM VITAE PRECOR OMNES INTROVENITE
PER ME TRANSIBVNT QVI COELI GAVDIA QVAERVNT
VIRGINE QVI NATVS NVLLO DE PATRE CREATVS
INTRANTES SALVET REDEVNTES IPSE GVBERNET

(from the Church of St.George in Milan, around Christ's monogram)

*(I am the door to life: everyone must enter;*
*all those searching for the joys of Heaven must enter through me;*
*May the One who was born from the Virgin, not from man,*
*Save everyone who enters, sustain those who return.)*

# The Door as a Symbol

*C*hurch doors always had a specific role and symbolism in the liturgy, which helps to understand the meaning of the Holy Door's opening ceremony. Books of liturgy and works of art have always emphasised this symbolism, from antiquity on to the present day.

The door of a church marks the division between sacred and profane, separating the church's interior from the outside world. It is the boundary defining welcome and exclusion. To anyone entering God's House, the door says: this is the house of God, this is the door to Heaven. Therefore, in crossing this threshold you must leave outside everything that is not worthy of God, taking on a respectful attitude towards everyone who lives in this house, and towards the sacred mysteries that are present here in the liturgy and the sacraments.

To maintain this respectful attitude, ever since the earliest centuries a "guard" stood at the entrance of churches, keeping the unworthy outside. Originally deacons had this task. Then it was given to ostiaries, who were encouraged by the bishop to keep watch "over the sanctity of the church with their word and their example, keeping the devil out of the invisible dwelling within the hearts of the faithful, opening it only to God."

*E*ven in the earliest churches, doors were an integral part of the decoration. They were ornamented, blessed and consecrated. On feast days, the doors were decorated with flowers and laurel leaves, a sign of worship. People would kneel on the threshold of the basilica and kiss the doors.

Paolino, Bishop of Nola, tells us that this used to happen in the Basilica of S.Felice. During the liturgical year, some rites were held in the doorways of churches: for example, on Palm Sunday the procession of Christ the King entered the church, which symbolised the city of Jerusalem, only after the door to the temple had been opened. On Holy Thursday, penitents were welcomed back into the community at church door, and weddings were officiated "in faciem Ecclesiae", in the doorway of the church, where the priest witnessed the couple's consent.

*S*ince church doors were so important, it has always been a major concern that they be made of high-quality materials and splendidly decorated, particularly in the main churches. Quite a few of these doors still survive, made of bronze, silver and wood. They are scattered throughout Europe, in Aix-la-Chapelle, Cologne, Hildesheim, Gniezno and, of course, in Italy. Memorable among these are the doors of S.Zeno in Verona, of the duomos of Pisa and Benevento, S.Michele al Gargano, the Baptistry of St.John in Florence, Monreale and Ravello.

Rome in particular has a unique series of superb doors, dating from between the second and the twentieth centuries.

Some of the oldest of these doors come from pagan monuments: for example, the Pantheon's bronze door is from Hadrian's time (117-138). The Lateran's main door comes from the Curia in the Forum. And the door of the Basilica of SS.Cosma e Damiano originally belonged to the Temple of Romulus.

*Memorable are also the doors of S.Sabina, in cypress wood (fifth century) and of the Lateran basilica and baptistery (fifth century; Pope Hillary). The oldest door in St.Paul's outside the Walls is from the eleventh century. It was commissioned by the abbot Hildebrand (future Pope Gregory VIII), and was restored after the 1823 fire by John XXIII and Paul VI. It is a fine example of the heights reached by Byzantine art at that time. Another door of this basilica, begun in 1931 by A. Maraini, has twelve panels with scenes from the Roman life of the apostles Peter and Paul, patron saints of Rome. S.Maria Maggiore also has a new door, dated 1949. It is by Ludovico Pugliaghi and represents the Incarnation. In St.Peter's there is a door by Filarete, a Door of the Dead by Giacomo Manzù, a Sacraments Door by V.Crocetti, a Door of Good and Evil by L.Minguzzi and a Prayer Door by L.Scorzelli.*

*From this brief outline, one can get an idea of how important doors were to God's temple, where his people enter and meet in the Lord.*

# Standing in Front of St. Peter's Holy Door

*S in and mercy. The message imparted by the Holy Door to anyone standing in front of it before entering the Basilica is central to the Gospels: the message that God's mercy reaches out to mankind's frailty.*

*The Holy Door does not commit this message to mere words, but uses images impressed in bronze. The door's twelve panels are like verses of a hymn, singing the mysteries of God's infinite mercy. They start out with scenes where man is debased by sin, then they show man's rehabilitation through repentance. The certainty of God's forgiveness provides enlightenment in every scene.*

## The Holy Door's Themes

*T he episodes shown on the door start from Adam's sin at the beginning of mankind's history, followed by scenes from the life of Jesus, who in his mercy came searching for what had been lost. The sources used are the Gospels and the Acts of the Apostles. In the last panel, Pope Pius XII is shown opening the door of mercy to suffering humanity in 1950, so that every man and woman of all time may rejoice in God's forgiveness and in returning to the House of God.*

*The imagery used in each scene is direct and immediate, speaking to both eyes and heart. Gregory the Great tells us that anyone can understand these episodes, even people who cannot read.*

*According to him, images are actually put in churches for the illiterate:"... ut hi qui litteras nesciunt saltem in parietibus videndo legant quae legere in codicibus non valent" (Ep. 208 of Gregory the Great to the Bishop of Marseilles).*

*To make the message clearer, each panel has a caption.*

*The meaning is rendered by a brief quote from the Bible, full of implications for the Christian way of life.*

*These are the images and the captions accompanying them.*

1    THE ANGEL AT THE GATES OF PARADISE.
2    THE FALL
      *Quod Heva tristis abstulit* (The joy that Eve took away)
3    MARY: THE ANNUNCIATION
      *Tu reddis almo germine* (You give back with your divine Son)
4    THE ANGEL OF THE ANNUNCIATION.
5    CHRIST'S BAPTISM IN THE JORDAN
      *Tu venis ad me?* (You come tu me?)
6    THE LOST SHEEP
      *Salvare quod perierat* (Saving what had been lost)
7    THE MERCIFUL FATHER
      *Pater, peccavi in coelum et coram te* (Father, I have sinned against heaven and against you)
8    THE CURE OF A PARALYTIC
      *Tolle grabatum tuum et ambula* (Get up, pick up your stretcher and walk)
9    THE WOMAN WHO WAS A SINNER
      *Remittuntur ei peccata multa* (Her sins, many as they are, have been forgiven her)
10   THE NEED FOR FORGIVENESS
      *Septuagies septies* (Seventy-seven times)
11   PETER'S DENIAL
      *Conversus Dominus respexit Petrum* (And the Lord turned and looked straight at Peter)
12   IN FRONT OF THE CRUCIFIX: THE GOOD THIEF
      *Hodie mecum eris in paradiso* (Today you will be with me in Paradise)
13   THE APPEARANCE TO THOMAS
      *Beati qui crediderunt* (Blessed are those who believe)
14   CHRIST'S APPEARANCE TO HIS DISCIPLINES
      *Accipite Spiritum Sanctum* (Receive the Holy Spirit)
15   THE CONVERSION OF SAUL
      *Sum Jesus quem tu persequeris* (I am Jesus, who you are persecuting)
16   OPENING THE HOLY DOOR
      *Sto ad ostium et pulso* (Look, I am standing at the door, knocking)

*Two latin inscriptions run across the bottom of the door: one gives details of the door's history and the other expresses the wish that anyone crossing this threshold may be rewarded with spiritual riches.*

Epigraph (a): *left side*
PIVS XII PONT. MAX. ANNO INEVNTE
SACRO MCML AENEIS HVIVS PORTAE
VALVIS VATICANAM BASILICAM DECO-
RARI IVSSIT LVDOVICO KAAS PETRIA-
NI TEMPLI OPERVM CVRATORE

*Pius XII Pontifex Maximus as the Holy Year 1950 drew near, ordered Ludovico Kaas, curator of Peter's temple, to adorn the Vatican Basilica with the bronze panels of this Holy Door.*

Epigraph (b): *right side*
HINC VBERES SCATEANT DIVINAE GRA-
TIAE LATICES OMNIVMQVE INGREDIEN-
TIVM ANIMOS EXPIENT ALMA REFI-
CIANT PACE CHRISTIANA VIRTVTE
EXORNENT ANNO SACRO MCML+

*From here the waters of divine grace flow abundantly, may they purify the soul of anyone who enters, restoring their spirit with divine peace and adorning them with Christian virtue. Holy Year, 1950.*

# THE ANGEL AT THE GATES OF PARADISE

*"God banished the man, and in front of the garden of Eden he posted the great winged creatures and the fiery flashing sword, to guard the way to the tree of life"* (Gen 3:24).

In the first panel of the Holy Door one sees the tree of knowledge in the lower left hand corner, entwined by the serpent, who tempted the woman to disobey God. The woman *"saw that the tree was good to eat and pleasing to the eye, and that it was enticing for the wisdom that it could give. So she took some of its fruit and ate it. She also gave some to her husband who was with her and he ate it. Then the eyes of both of them were opened..."* (Gen 3:6).

Above this, in the middle section, is a flying angel. It holds a flaming sword, given to him by God to protect the path leading to the tree of knowledge. The angel extends his left arm, pointing the way out of Paradise to Adam and Eve. Never again will they be allowed into that fertile and wonderful place which God had prepared for them, both to live in and as a sacred place which he could share

with the beings he created. The angel's index finger points towards infinity, towards time and the profound need to redeem time.

Even the angel's hair is blowing in the tempest of evil, which has broken over man and all of nature. For nature also has been touched by the curse of original sin! Outside of Paradise, a dry shrub bears witness to the consequences of sin.

God's word leave no doubt about this:"...*accursed be the soil because of you! Painfully will you get your food from it as long as you live. It will yield you brambles and thistles as you eat the produce of the land. By the sweat of your face will you earn your food...*"(Gen 3:17-19).

Even the animals are shown fleeing in terror: from this moment onwards, wild instincts will awaken in them and they will no longer be man's friend, but always ready to unleash their fury on mankind.

The complete happiness enjoyed by our ancestors has been destroyed. The integrity of nature, God's spiritual friendship and his rich gifts are a thing of the past.

Punishment extends to all of Adam's descendants, who will inherit the burden and consequences of original sin until the end of time. This loss of grace has made everyone eternally poor!

After describing the temptation and fall of man, the writer has God say in bitter irony: "*Now the man has become like one of us in knowing good from evil...*".

From that day onwards, a long history of suffering began, lightened only the hope that salvation would come, as God had said it would in the very hour of condemnation. God had in fact said to the serpent: "*I shall put enmity between you and the woman, and between your offspring and hers...*"(Gen 3:15). A man born of woman will overcome Satan and be the most eminent member of the human family, as well as its saviour.

This hope of salvation was kept alive by the prophets until the fullness of time arrived. During the waiting period, Eve, who was "sad...", never ceased gazing through darkness towards this luminous moment of the future which would lift the shadows of original sin: "*May this woman come quickly, the earth open and the Saviour be born.*"

# THE FALL
## QVOD HEVA TRISTIS ABSTVLIT (The joy that Eve took away)

*"So Yahweh God expelled man from the garden of Eden, to till the soil from which he had been taken."* (Gen 3:23).

The second panel shows our ancestors being cast out of Paradise.

Adam is bent under the weight of God's curse, and leans forward, almost falling over. God's image is shattered, but his presence, symbolised by a cloud, still sustains man.

Adam looks over his shoulder, his face expressing the anguish of losing Paradise.

His left hand also is extended backwards, opened as if to ward off the blow of God's punishment.

His right hand is raised, expressing hope in the salvation promised by God.

Eve, the first woman, hides her face in shame. Tears run down her cheeks. She covers her face with the same arm that picked the fruit from the tree.

Eve listened to the serpent's ambiguous talk. She

believed him, though he was lying and could not keep his promise. She gave her husband the forbidden fruit. Eve is the cause of death. This is why sadness follows her.

These are the most important beings created by God, and the gate to Paradise lies behind them. They are leaving it barefoot, and will have to walk on an accursed soil covered with brambles and thistles, which will yield food only through the sweat of their brow.

Everyone is involved in the fall, from Adam onwards; the contamination of original sin flows through the ages: "*it was through one man that sin came into the world, and through sin, death...*". But there is hope for the future: "*Adam prefigured the One who was to come*"(Rom 5:12-14).

Adam now is each one of us. The first two panels are therefore about original sin, summing up the situation and foretelling redemption. Their message is: "*Quod Heva tristis, abstulit, tu reddis almo germine...*" (the joy that Eve took away is given back to us through your son...).

These lines come from "O gloriosa Domina...", a hymn most probably written by the bishop of Poitiers, Venanzio Fortunato, between the seventh and eighth century. Venanzio knew that original sin lay heavily on womankind, but he saw a connection between Mary and Eve.

Through her son, Mary brought back into the world what had been lost by Eve through original sin. Woman's responsibility in the fall had already been pointed out in the past, and the memory of original sin, caused by the first woman, increased their condition of inferiority.

St.Ambrose, in a wonderful chapter of "De institutione Virginis", proves that it is easier to excuse womankind for original sin than man. Eve, he writes, was seduced by an angel (even though a fallen one), and she repented more quickly and more generously, accusing the serpent, not Adam. A woman also made up for that first sin by giving birth to our Saviour. Ambrose then concludes: "*Come close, Eve, who are now called Mary; you give us an example of virginity and give us a God; this God visited just one woman, but welcomes them all*" (St.Ambrose, De institutione Virginis, c.V).

# MARY: THE ANNUNCIATION

## TV REDDIS ALMO GERMINE (You give back with your divine Son)

*"The angel Gabriel was sent by God to a town in Galilee called Nazareth, to a virgin betrothed to a man named Joseph. The virgin's name was Mary. He went in and said to her: "Rejoice, you who enjoy God's favour! The Lord is with you". She was deeply disturbed by these words and asked herself what this greeting could mean, but the angel said to her:"Mary, do not be afraid; you have won God's favour. Look! You are to conceive in your womb and bear a son, and you must name him Jesus..."*
*(Lk 1:26-31).*

This is how Luke begins to tell the story of Christ's incarnation. The panels showing Adam and Eve's fall and the annunciation are close together, running parallel on the Holy Door.

The theme of expulsion from Paradise and the closure of its gates is balanced by the mystery of Paradise re-opening. Eve, the cause of sin and of Adam's downfall, is set beside Mary, whose perfect submission to God's will brings into the world the embodiment of life itself. In Paradise, Adam and Eve's arrogance caused the decay of all humanity; in Nazareth, Mary's serene humanity started the process of redemption.

The liturgy says: *"Quod Heva tristis abstulit, tu reddis almo germinare: intrent ut astra flebiles, coeli recludis cardines"* (the joy that Eve took away is given back to us through your son: and the path to the

Kingdom of Heaven is opened). The gates of Heaven open and mankind heads towards salvation.

This image of the Annunciation has none of the porticos seen in four-teenth century and Renaissance paintings; Mary's room has the intimate atmosphere of Flemish art, with a window framing her head and opening up onto the countryside. Mary wears a "maphorium" (mantle) and sits on a high-backed bench, spiritually absorbed, her hands joined in prayer, and showing a delicate profile. She is contemplating the mystery already foretold by the book of Scriptures open on a stand, which the angel is now revealing to her. Mary praying, filled with the power of the Holy Spirit, takes the place of Eve: the Mother of God obliterates the first mother of mankind, who fled from God. Nazareth becomes the dawn of salvation, the beginning of freedom from sin and death, which had come into being at the beginning of mankind's history. Everything occurs through the Holy Spirit. The angel calls Mary "full of grace", but she refers to herself as "the Lord's servant". God asked Mary to collaborate in man's salvation, and she agreed, thus making it possible for the Lord to become a man. Mary, as the first person delivered from sin, heads the host of people entering the gates of Heaven.

She helps them along the way, helping them overcome the difficulties along their path (*iter para tutum*) and to let go of the distracting charms of living creatures.

This is why the church refers to Mary as *"Ianua coeli"* (the door to Heaven), *"pervia coeli porta"* (Heaven's open door) and *"Felix coeli porta"* (the happy door to Heaven).

We salute Mary, in front of the Holy Door, as the entrance to light, and thank her for continuing to radiate the light she herself received, for the benefit of every person who is looking for God.

# THE ANGEL OF THE ANNUNCIATION

*"The angel Gabriel was sent by God...to a virgin whose name was Mary. He went in and said to her: "Rejoice, you who enjoy God's favour! The Lord is with you". She was deeply disturbed by these words and asked herself what this greeting could mean..."*
*(Lk 1:26-29).*

The Holy Door panel on the annunciation shows the Angel hovering vertically in the air, a traditional pose of antique iconography. In a later period, from the twelfth century onwards, the Angel is usually kneeling. Some mystics (such as the author of the Meditations of Pseudo-Bonaventure) imagine that Mary also knelt after encountering the Angel, as they both adored the Word made flesh.
On the Holy Door, the angel standing at the gates of Paradise with a flaming sword has its counterpart in another angel, dressed with sober elegance and with the beautiful name of Gabriel.
He approaches a simply-dressed woman, speaking to her in the name of God. He calls her "full of grace", words never used before for any living being, and all the angels are overshadowed by her splendour.

Her dignity sets her above all creation. *"The Lord is with you"*: she has been chosen by God to start the process of salvation, which will continue through her. She will conceive a child and give birth: he will be her son and the son of God. He will save man from evil, he will be Christ the Saviour.

He will be called the Son of God and he will have a kingdom which will not end.

Every day the Church and the faithful take up the Angel's greeting, repeating that "ave" frequently. It is recited three times a day in the Angelus Domini, in the morning, at midday and in the evening, bringing the mystery of the incarnation and of redemption into everyday life.

This particular angel holds a rose in its hand, an offering to Mary. The Angel was always shown in antiquity bearing a gift.

For centuries this gift was the *baculus viatoris* used by emperors' messengers, a long metal rod with an ornament on top. Later on, the Angel was shown carrying a branch of evergreen, a symbol of peace between God and man (see Simone Martini's "Annunciation" in the Uffizi Gallery in Florence).

During the Middle Ages the branch became a lily, offered humbly by the Angel to his queen, a sign of her absolute purity. At the same time, the liturgy sang: "...you will conceive a child, but you will remain a virgin" *(concipies Filium et eris mater semper intacta)*.

Other floral gifts include a pot of flowers placed on the floor between the Angel and Mary (see Simone Martini, Filippo Lippi; the theme was also used by Consorti in the previous panel).

It had a specific meaning: flowers symbolise spring, which is when the annunciation occurred. They are also a symbol of Nazareth and Bernard of Clairvaux wrote that *"the flower (Jesus) was born from a flower (Mary), in a flower (Nazareth, during the flower season (spring)."*

# CHRIST'S BAPTISM IN THE JORDAN

## TV VENIS AD ME? (You come to me?)

*"Then Jesus appeared: he came from Galilee to the Jordan to be baptised by John. John tried to dissuade him, with the words, "It is I who need baptism from you, and yet you come to me!" But Jesus replied, "Leave it like this for the time being; it is fitting that we should, in this way, do all that uprightness demands". Then John gave in to him." (Mt 3, 13-15)*

Crowds of people gather on the banks of the river Jordan to see John the Baptist, hear him speak and be baptised by him. One day, Jesus comes from Galilee and stands in line to be baptised. But John doesn't want to baptise him! For John had declared that he was not the Messiah. He was less than a slave to the Messiah; according to the customs of the time, a slave tied his master's sandals, and John was not even worthy of this in his estimation. *"You come to me?"* There is an implicit awareness in this question that Jesus is untouched by sin. He is the Lamb of God, who takes away the sins of the world. In his answer, *"it is fitting that we should, in this way, do all that uprightness demands"*, Jesus makes it clear that he is humbling himself in the rite of baptism to conform to God's will, and this will indicates that Christ's destiny is one of service and sacrifice. In this episode on the Holy Door, Jesus is standing in the Jor-

dan river. According to the liturgy, from that moment onwards all the waters of the earth were sanctified. Whenever water is poured out in baptism, everyone touched by it will be born to a new life in the name of the Father, the Son and the Holy Spirit. The water of purification frees mankind from original sin, as well as every other sin. The water of enlightenment: anyone washing in it comes back to life from the darkness of sin and is illuminated by Christ. As St.Ambrose said: *"We carry Christ in our hearts like the midday sun"*. The water of salvation and life. No baptised person can drown, no tempest can ever shake the vessel of life. In baptism, Christ gives us back much more than we ever lost through Adam. The cross eliminates sin, and God shares his gifts with us.

This is the work of the Holy Spirit. When Jesus was baptised, "he at once came up from the water, and suddenly the heavens opened and he saw the spirit of God descending like a dove and coming down on him. And suddenly there was a voice from Heaven, *"This is my Son, my Beloved; my favour rests on him."* (Mt 3:17). On the Holy Door, Christ is in the Jordan and the Baptist's hand pours water on his head. A dove over Christ's head symbolises the presence of the Holy Spirit and Christ's intimate communion with God, sealing his mission on earth. Two writers teach us how to experience the mystery of Christ' baptism. This is Gregory of Nissa's suggestion: *"Today Christ has received baptism from John, so that everything stained may be purified. The Holy Spirit has come down to lift mankind up to Heaven, to raise the fallen and to humiliate he who had caused man to fall."* A prayer of the Ambrosian liturgy puts this mystery into everyday life: *"O Eternal Lord, you revealed yourself to us on the Jordan river, making your voice resonate like thunder, pointing us towards the Saviour who came down from Heaven, and showing us that you are the Father of uncreated light. The Heavens opened and you blessed the air, purified the waters, manifesting the presence of your only Son through the Holy Spirit, in the form of a dove. Now the waters have received your blessing and they have washed away our curse. Now all believers can be purified of sin and God may have his adopted children in eternal life.All those born to life and time, prey to death with the complicity of sin, can now be welcomed into grace and brought back to the glory of the Kingdom of Heaven"* (Ambrosian Preface to the Epiphany).

# THE LOST SHEEP
## SALVARE QVOD PERIERAT (Saving what had been lost)

*"Which one of you with a hundred sheep, if he lost one, would fail to leave the ninety-nine in the desert and go after the missing one til he found it? And when he found it, would he not joyfully take it on his shoulders and then, when he got home, call together his friends and neighbours, saying to them, "Rejoice in me, I have found my sheep that was lost." In the same way, I tell you, there will be more rejoicing in heaven over one sinner repenting than over ninety-nine upright people who have no need for repentance."* (Lk 15:4-7).

The sixth and seventh panel show two of Luke's three parables on mercy, taken from the fifteenth chapter of his Gospel. They are the sublime revelation of God's heart. Gregory the Great once exclaimed about these three parables (the lost sheep, the lost drachma and the prodigal son), *"Disce con Dei in verbis Dei"*, meaning "Learn to know the heart of God through his Word".

The parables were told in this context: Jesus was sharing a meal with tax collectors and sinners, two catagories of people who usually were not close to God and his laws. The fact that Jesus welcomes them causes an outcry among the more conventional Jews. Jesus answers them by proclaiming the infinite mercy of God, saying that Heaven overflows with joy when sinners repent.

God is often described in the Bible as a shepherd

looking after his people, who are seen as a flock of sheep. In the Gospels, Christ says that he is a shepherd, looking for lost sheep. The shepherd leads his flock back to the fold, only to discover when he counts them that one sheep is missing: it had gotten lost and fallen into a ravine. So the shepherd climbs down into the deep gorge, and when he finds the sheep he doesn't punish it but frees it from a tangle of thistles and brambles, and carries the wounded animal back home on his shoulders. *"Quarens me sedisti lassus, ...tantus labor non sit cassus"* (Looking for me, you sat down wearily..., that so much hardship might not be vain). God's joy over the conversion of a sinner does not distort his justice, but expresses his desire to help anyone who has strayed.

The shepherd on the Holy Door has both arms outstretched, breaking the panel up crosswise, and his hands have been torn by rocks and brambles. The opened arms express God's welcome to anyone needing salvation and the hardships the shepherd bears symbolise God's determination to complete this task. He came "to save what had been lost".

During the Julibee, St.Peter reminds us that we too are lost sheep, who have strayed from the fold and from the watchful care of our shepherd. But this is the right time to return *"to the shepherd and guardian of your souls"* (see 1 P 2:25).

What awaits the returning sheep? The Lord says: *"I myself shall pasture my sheep, I shall give them rest"* (Ezk 34:15).

# THE MERCIFUL FATHER

PATER, PECCAVI IN COELVM ET CORAM TE (Father, I have sinned against heaven and against you)

*"There was a man who had two sons. The younger said to his father, 'Father, let me have the share of my estate that will come to me...'. The younger son got together everything he had and left for a distant country where he squandered his money on a life of debauchery. When he had spent it all, he began to feel the pinch...then he came to his senses... so he left the place and went back to his father. When he was still a long way off, his father saw him and was moved to pity. He ran to the boy, clasped him in his arms and kissed him...The father said, '...we will celebrate by having a feast, because this son of mine was dead and he has come back to life; he was lost and is found..."* (Lk 15, 11-24).

For centuries, this parable was been called the prodigal son. Then it seemed better to call it the parable of the merciful father. The hero of the story is in fact the father, not the son. The three protagonists, a father and his two sons, are described in a few words.

We feel especially close to the father and our imagination is full of his gestures and words. He also fills the central space of the Holy Door panel, standing beside his well and welcoming his son, who has finally come home. Nature itself rejoices, in the form a dog, a horse and some palm trees.

Jesus gradually unveils the father's qualities in the parable: he is the image of God, whose love has always existed and always will. The depth of this love is almost incomprehensible, and can be understood only if one thinks of a merciful God, who is patient

and forgiving. The son demands his share of inheritance, coldly and calculatingly, and the father gives in to him, complying with a law which allows the youngest son a third of his father's estate. The father knows his inheritance will be squandered in a life of debauchery, indifferent to God's commandments, but he respects his son's decision.

The father waits until his son's ruinous course is halted, and he finally turns back from the path of misery and desperation. When the father sees him arriving in the distance, he takes pity on his son. Forgetting his dignity and age, he runs towards him, embracing him and kissing him tenderly, not even allowing the son to complete the confession he had prepared.

The father welcomes the son, honouring him as if he were a king, with gestures which only a loving father would think of. He is given a robe, the highest honour, and a ring, symbolising his rehabilitation and their renewed trust.

The sandals placed on his feet are a sign of his recovered freedom, because slaves walked barefoot.

Then the father wants to celebrate his son's return. For what reason? Because a dead man has come back to life, and he who was lost has been found. God is a true father, with a vast family. Even if one of his children rebels against him and causes him great sorrow, God does not forget that child: God loves each one of us, as if we were the only one he loves.

# THE CURE OF A PARALYTIC

## TOLLE GRABATVM TVVM ET AMBVLA (Get up, pick up your stretcher and walk)

*"When he returned to Capernaum, some time later word went round that he was in the house, and so many people collected that there was no room left, even in front of the door... Some people came bringing him a paralytic carried by four men... Seeing their faith, Jesus said to the paralytic, 'My child, your sins are forgiven... But to prove to you that the Son of man has authority to forgive sins on earth - he said to the paralytic - I order you: get up, pick up your stretcher, and go off home...'" (Mk 2:1-3, 5, 10-11).*

Jesus is in Capernaum, probably in Peter's house. Since many people have gathered, he begins to preach the Word to them. In such a crowd, four people have a hard time bringing the paralytic to see Jesus, and they are forced to lower the stretcher down from the roof. This is a sign of their determination, but also of their faith. Jesus tells the paralytic that God has forgiven his sins, which according to Jewish credence are the cause of his illness. He is thereby giving hope to the sick man: if God can forgive his sins, then he can also get well.

This situation is repeated during Holy Year, and is especially topical in Peter's house, meaning the Basilica of St.Peter's. Everyone's sins can be forgiven. Redemption becomes real and must then continue to work in each one of us and throughout the world. The Kingdom of God can begin again, with

a greater stability.

In this panel of the Holy Door, we see the very moment when the paralytic starts to stand, as he is drawn upwards by the power in Christ's hands.

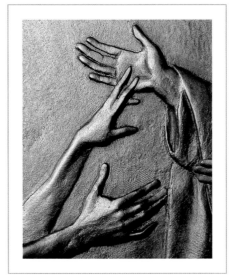

The miracle throws light on the mystery of Christ.

This time he is not among sick people: Jesus has always been very sensitive to man's suffering. He has seen pain and wanted to alleviate it, liberating its victims. As Peter told Cornelius and his pagan friends in Caesarea, *"because God was with him, Jesus went about doing good and curing all who had fallen into the power of the devil"(Ac 10:38).*

Sick people gather around Jesus in every moment of the day and in every occasion, and he frees them from physical suffering. But he heals their illnesses to liberate their conscience from sin's mortal sickness.

Christ's work goes on to this day, though now of course people are not cured miraculously like the paralytic was, without healing rigid joints and atrophied muscles. The Redeemer's saving power endures, and even when an illness is not cured by prayer, one must still believe that he saves us and that the illness has a meaning, mysteriously completing the Passion of Christ.

Whatever role a Christian may have within the Church, when he or she alleviate the suffering of sick people they are continuing Christ's work. This is the gift each one of us hopes for when we are sick in body and spirit, and it is a gift which every Christian may offer his fellow man. In looking after a sick person, we make Christ present. We are the tangible part of the mysterious presence of the Son of God, who succours a sick portion of his mystic body.

In the face of this miracle, a paralytic man restored to health and strong enough to carry his own stretcher (*"...pick up your stretcher, and go off home..."*), Christians are moved to proclaim their faith, joining voices in God's praise: "We have never seen anything like this".

However, some people in the name of religious obedience, do not accept this revelation of God's merciful love and oppose his project for salvation.

# THE WOMAN WHO WAS A SINNER

REMITTVNTVR EI PECCATA MVLTA (Her sins, many as they are, have been forgiven her)

*"One of the Pharisees invited him to a meal. When he arrived in the Pharisee's house and took his place at table, suddenly a woman came in who had a bad name in the town...she had brought with her an alabaster jar of ointment. She waited behind him at his feet, weeping, and her tears fell on his feet, and she wiped them away with her hair; then she covered his feet with kisses and anointed them with ointment. When the Pharisee who had invited him saw this, he said to himself, "If this man were a prophet, he would know who this woman is...".*
*Then Jesus said to her; "Your sins are forgiven...go in peace."*
*(Lk 7:36-39; 48, 50).*

The moving story about a woman who had sinned ("who had a bad name in that town") begins with Jesus at a banquet. He never refuses invitations because they are opportunities to convert sinners, bringing God to his people in need, giving them joy and announcing the Messiah's coming. In this panel of the Holy Door one sees Simon the Pharisee, a typical practising Jew who respects every minor detail of the law and despises anyone less diligent than himself. He has invited Jesus to dine with him because he is a celebrity and it is an honour to be his host; it is also an opportunity to observe Jesus at close range.

This woman was known to everyone by virtue of her trade. She probably came to see Jesus because she had met him before, hearing him speak compassionately even to fallen women; she knew that he was a friend of sinners. Something had touched her heart and made

her seek out this prophet. For she considered him a prophet! But for other people the issue wasn't that simple. These other people felt that a master, as the Jews considered Jesus, shouldn't waste his time teaching law to a woman. To a woman who moreover had a bad reputation. They were all astonished at the way she behaved with Jesus. When the woman drew near him, she actually started crying. She knelt at his feet, wetting them with her tears and using her hair to dry them. Then she took a jar of precious ointment, the kind that every woman carried with her, and poured it on Christ's feet, kissing them.

Jesus, who was good and merciful, did not push the woman aside, but showed respect for her dignity.

The Pharisee behaved quite differently. Politeness forced him to make no outward sign of disapproval, but he began to doubt that Jesus was actually a prophet. And, as St.Augustine said, *"Jesus heard Simon's thoughts"*, so he told him the parable of the two men in debt. All men are in debt: some have small debts, like Simon, who thought that he was above criticism. And some have big debts, like the woman of this story, who knew that her debt with God was grievous. God, in his infinite mercy, is willing to forgive everyone, and particularly anyone who has loved him very much and trusted in his forgiveness.

The woman knows perfectly well what she has been saved from. Simon, on the other hand, is arrogantly pleased with himself and doesn't realise that he also needs to be saved from something. The woman knew that she needed forgiveness, while Simon thought that he was in the right.

One has to be aware of one's sins, meaning not just the more cumbersome sins, but also those small sins noticed only by those closest to us, and which cause unhappiness to many people and for far too long. Forgiveness of sins is in any case an act of God's mercy, when he relieves the sinner with his grace.

The emptiness of human misery is filled by love and faith. *"Your faith has saved you; go in peace"*.

In this panel the banquet table divides the people into two groups. Jesus is in the foreground, with his arms extended to welcome the woman at his feet. Two other people are in the background; one of them is Simon, who watches the scene doubtfully.

# THE NEED FOR FORGIVENESS
## SEPTVAGIES SEPTIES (Seventy-seven times)

*"Then Peter went up to him and said, 'Lord, how often must I forgive my brother if he wrongs me? As often as seven times?' Jesus answered, 'Not seven, I tell you, but seventy-seven times'"* (Mt 18:21-22).

Peter often asked Jesus questions, and the answers he received seemed to have the intention of preparing the apostle for his future duties. On this occasion, Jesus had just finished talking about brotherly correction, saying that we are morally obliged to admonish a brother who does something wrong, helping him to change his ways. Peter's question is about forgiving someone who has personally injured us: *"how often must I forgive my brother if he wrongs me? As often as seven times?"*. Peter confidently assumed that this was a generous estimate, since in Judaic law one could only be forgiven three times for the same offence. If the offence was repeated a fourth time, then there was no obligation of forgiveness. Therefore, in asking Jesus if forgiving seven times was enough, Peter had amply surpassed the limits of tolerance preached by the rab-

bis, and could well assume that he had reached true perfection. But Jesus corrects him: one must forgive *"seventy-seven times"*. Jesus was not talking about arithmetic. He meant that forgiveness should not be limited: one must forgive everything, always, and each time our fellow man needs this forgiveness. Instead of a mathematical calculation, Jesus suggests a complete change of attitude, which entails unlimited forgiveness, like the infinite mercy of God. No matter what the injury may be, we must always offer our fellow man sincere forgiveness, just as God forgives each one of us.

To make this teaching clear and help his disciples remember it, Jesus tells the parable of the unforgiving debtor. The king had cancelled this man's substantial debt, yet he pitilessly insisted in being paid by his fellow-servant, and his hardness towards others gets punished.

The message of this parable is clear: if we are incapable of forgiveness, then we cannot hope to be forgiven by God. It is our duty to forgive, and we must tirelessly fulfil this duty, without any restrictions. Forgiving as God forgives: he is never tired of our weaknesses.

I move away from this panel, carrying in my heart Christ's

words, *"Blessed are the merciful, they shall have mercy shown them"* *(Mt 5:7)*. In my heart are the words of his prayer, *"And forgive us our debts, as we have forgiven those who are in debt with us"* *(Mt 6:12)*. Let us listen the great words of Ben Sira, who already two centuries before Christ advised, *"Pardon your neighbour any wrongs done to you, and when you pray, your sins will be forgiven. If anyone nurses anger against another, can one then demand compassion from the Lord?"* *(Si 28:2-3)*.

# PETER'S DENIAL

CONVERSVS DOMINVS RESPEXIT PETRVM (And the Lord turned and looked straight at Peter)

*"And the Lord turned and looked straight at Peter, and Peter remembered the Lord's words when he said to him, "Before the cock crows today, you will have disowned me three times.! And he went outside and wept bitterly." (Lk 22:61-62).*

The moment of Christ's passion was a moment of bitter sorrow for Peter. He had sworn that he was willing to die for his master, and this master was now suffering. The Passion was the darkest hour of Peter's life, and he was never able to forget it: on that night, he disowned Jesus.

He had not stayed awake on the Mount of Olives, to watch over his anguished master. Peter had a brief moment of clumsy courage in Gethsemane, when he used his sword on Malchus and was admonished by Jesus, *"Put your sword back, for all who draw the sword will die by the sword..."*. Then Peter ran away with the other disciples, leaving Jesus alone with his enemies. When his panic had subsided, Peter followed Christ to the high priest's house, accompanied by John. And when a woman recognised him in the firelight as Christ's follower, Peter trembled and denied it.

He repeated the denial a second and a third time, swearing that it was not true, his tongue loosened by fear.

The Gospels tell us that after that moment of weakness, Peter repented and went back to the Lord.

A fortunate coincidence occurred. Jesus was dragged out of the court-room to where Peter stood, in an enclosure. Passing in front of his friend, Jesus looked straight into his eyes (Lk 22:61). It was an infinitely sad look. It was as powerful as a miracle: even at the moment of our Lord's annihilation, he guided world events and the lives of individuals.

Memory struck Peter then: during the Last Supper, Jesus had foretold that the cock would crow at the same time of Peter's betrayal. With a deeply troubled heart and weeping bitterly, Peter ran out of that enclosure, repenting the injury he had done to his master.

When Pope Leo used to describe this scene to the faithful during the Passion ceremony in St.Peter's, he always remarked, *"Peter was destined to be the pastor of the Church, and he had to learn mercy for others through his own sin. God first allowed Peter know himself and then made him a leader, so that through his own weakness he learned to feel compassion for the weakness of others."*

The scene on the Holy Door shows the encounter between Jesus and Peter. The palace of Caiaphas can be seen in the background. Christ's hands are tied: his imprisonment frees everyone from the fetters of sin, which destroys mankind. His face and his gaze are turned towards Peter, who is weeping in repentance for what he has done, and covers his face with his hands. From that night onwards, and according to tradition every night, Peter would wake up at cock's crow and weep over that denial of Christ, which was always alive in his memory. He says to us: every sin that we regret, God forgives. The cock shown at the top of the panel also appears in the liturgy, particularly in the morning hymns, *"Preco diei iam sonat noctis profundae pervigil... hoc, ipse petra ecclesiae, canendo culpam diluit"* (St.Ambrose, Hymn of Sunday Lauds). (The vigilant cock crows already in the deep of the night; Peter, hearing him, weeps bitter tears).

# IN FRONT OF THE CRUCIFIX *THE GOOD THIEF*

HODIE MECVM ERIS IN PARADISO (Today you will be with me in Paradise)

*"When they reached the place called The Skull, there they crucified him and the two criminals, one on his right, the other on his left... One of the criminals hanging there abused him... But the other spoke up and rebuked him... Then he said, 'Jesus, remember me when you come into your kingdom'. He answered him, 'In truth I tell you, today you will be with me in Paradise'"* (Lk 23:33, 39, 40, 42-43).

With this panel the Holy Door's narrative pauses in front of the twelfth station of the Cross, the station in which the crucified Jesus is flanked by two criminals. They are his companions in torment, assigned to him by human justice. Only these three figures can be seen on the panel. It shows none of the other people which the Gospels tell us were present on Calvary that day, between the sixth and ninth hour.

Luke's narrative describes a watching populace in the background, whose mood might have been indifference or perhaps surprise that God did not save his Son. The leaders, on the other hand, sneered at Jesus, goading him to miraculously free himself, and thereby prove that was the Christ of God, the Chosen One (see Lk 23:35). Even the soldiers joined this gruesome celebration, mocking the "King of the Jews".

Other people were also there: "All the friends of Jesus stood at a distance". How can one measure that distance? The attitude of these friends is hard to understand. They let their master die, surrounded by horrible bystanders. That "distance" weighs on the spirit.

The bystander closest to Jesus, who took up his defence, was one of the two criminals. They were common felons, sentenced by Roman justice to be crucified for their crimes. One of them joins the chorus of people abusing Christ in his suffering, while the other defends him, rebuking his companion for his impiety in the supreme moment of death. This man sensed that Jesus, who hung on the cross between them, was actually the Messiah, and so he asks to be remembered at the end of time, when the Kingdom of God will begin. Jesus answers his prayer: *"In truth I tell you, today you will be with me in Paradise"* (Lk 23:43). The thief asks to be saved at the end of all time, and Jesus perfects this request by telling him that salvation is already upon him, "today", at the moment of his death.

Bousset remarks, "His request to remembered has been answered to a superlative degree: today, what promptness; 'you will be with me', the most beautiful and complete communion; 'in Paradise', participating in Christ's blessed life, seated at the right hand of the Father". Augustine envied the thief: "He stole throughout his whole life, and at its end he stole Paradise". Every abyss of misery can be lit by God's mercy, which elevates us: *"From the depths I call to you, Yahweh: Lord, hear my cry... If you kept a record of our sins, Lord, who could stand their ground? But with you is forgiveness..."* (Ps 130:1, 3-4). Even in the final moments of his life, the good shepherd looks for the lost sheep.

The panel describes these two attitudes effectively: the good thief and Jesus gaze at one another, while the other condemned man turns his head away, refusing to see the One who died for everyone's sins.

# THE APPEARANCE TO THOMAS

BEATI QVI CREDIDERVNT (Blessed are those who believe)

*"Eight days later, the disciples were in the house again and Thomas was with them. The doors were closed, but Jesus came in and stood among them. 'Peace be with you', he said. Then he spoke to Thomas, 'Put your finger here; look, here are my hands. Give me your hand; put it in my side. Do not be unbelieving any more but believe.' Thomas replied, 'My God and my Lord!' Jesus said to him: 'You believe because you have seen me. Blessed are those who have not seen and yet believe.'"* (Jn 20:26-29).

After rising from the dead, Jesus appeared to his apostles on two occasions: on the night of the resurrection, when Thomas was absent, and eight days later, when he was present. The fact that Jesus appeared to them twice, underlines the importance that the apostles were to have in spreading the Paschal message. But Thomas wouldn't accept this message on faith. He insists on seeing Jesus before believing that he has risen from the dead, and the proof he receives is an important statement of the truth of the resurrection. As Gregory the Great wrote, *"God's infinite mercy provided that this disciple's need to touch the Master's wounds, also healed the wounds of our own incredulity. The answer to Thomas' doubts is more convincing than the faith of believers, because he only believes after receiving direct proof, and so our minds can overcome every uncertainty, confirming our faith..."* (St.Gregory the Great, Homely 26, 4-7). Jesus had already given some of his disciples the joy

of seeing him after the resurrection. He had appeared to Mary Magdalene, who the embodiment of love and devotion to Jesus, to whom she owed everything. He had shown himself to Peter, who was full of grief and penitence for having betrayed the Master. Jesus wanted to free Peter from the torment of his disloyalty towards one who had chosen him. He also met two of his followers, whose hearts faltered in despair, though they were still faithful to Jesus, ever present in their shattered world. After seeing him, the darkness in their souls became light. Jesus appeared to his apostles while they were at table; they were full of fear and despair, but still talked of him and loved him. And he appeared to Thomas, whose doubts sprang from the need to believe in and love his Lord, that Lord he wanted to offer his life to. Jesus asks Thomas to make sure of his Master's resurrection, using words spoken by Thomas eight days before to his fellow disciples: *"Put your finger here; look, here are my hands. Give me your hand; put it in my side..."*. Thomas replies, *"My Lord and my God!" (Jn 20:27)*. According to Scripture commentators, this is the most beautiful profession of faith in John's Gospel. The wording commits us, for that

adjective "my" says that we are God's people, that we have been saved. We belong to God and he belongs to us. *"Blessed are those who have not seen and yet believe!"*. It was a great privilege for the apostle to have heard, seen, contemplated and touched the Incarnate Word (*see* 1 Jn 1:1). Blessedness for us means accepting the personal testimony of the apostles, waiting patiently and humbly, learning even through torturous ways like that of Thomas, and finally affirming the creed, *"My Lord and my God"*.

# CHRIST'S APPEARANCE TO HIS DISCIPLINES

ACCIPITE SPIRITVM SANCTVM (Receive the Holy Spirit )

"*In the evening of that same day... Jesus came and stood among them. He said to them, 'Peace be with you,' and, after saying this, he showed them his hands and his side. The disciples were filled with joy at seeing the Lord, and he said to them again, 'Peace be with you. As the Father sent me, so I am sending you.' After saying this he breathed on them and said: 'Receive the Holy Spirit. If you forgive anyone's sins, they are forgiven; if you retain anyone's sins, they are retained.'*"
(*Jn 20:19, 20-23*).

Let us look at the Holy Door: the Resurrected Christ is shown surrounded by his apostles. He has just told them who he is and entrusted them with a mission: to go out in the world and spread forgiveness, sharing in God's unique capacity to pardon sins. These remarkable events took place on the night of Easter, while the apostles were gathered together at the same table where, only a few days previously, Jesus had celebrated the feast of Passover with them. On that occasion, Jesus had sealed his new Covenant with the sacrifice of his body and blood. But on Easter evening, the apostles sitting at supper were full of fear, and had carefully barred the door of the room. Jesus came in and greeted them in the usual Jewish way, saying "Peace be with you". To convince them of his identity, he showed them the wounds on his hands and in his side. The apos-

tles rejoiced at seeing the Lord.

To those who recognised him, Jesus granted peace and joy, his first Easter gifts.

Then Jesus gave his disciples a special mission, emphasising its similarity with his own mission: *"As the Father sent me, so I am sending you"*. The word "as" stands out, giving purpose to the apostles' task. They were to carry on the mission which God had entrusted to Jesus, making it the basis of their ministry, and using Christ as their ideal. This was the realisation of a prayer invoked by Jesus just a few days before, during the last supper: *"As you sent me into the world, I have sent them into the world..."* (*Jn 17:18*).

Christ's third gift was the gift of the Holy Spirit: *"...he breathed on them and said: Receive the Holy Spirit"*. The main purpose of this gift was to sanctify the apostles: they had to believe in Christ and give his personal testimony. They were given the Holy Spirit for a reason: so that they could forgive sins. This is the Resurrected Christ's most precious gift to his Church.

Forgiveness of sins, so that man can be reconciled man with God, is the apostles' goal: *"Receive the Holy Spirit.*

*If you forgive anyone's sins, they are forgiven; if you retain anyone's sins, they are retained"*. Through the Holy Spirit, and the sacrament of penance, a new humanity, free from evil, can come into being. The message that this panel of the Holy Door imparts, is that anyone passing through here must seek a reconciliation with God, by means of the Holy Spirit. For it is the Holy Spirit that grants "remissio omnium peccatorum", coming down to purify our consciences (Roman missal, Offertory prayer).

# THE CONVERSION OF SAUL

SVM JESVS QVEM TV PERSEQVERIS (I am Jesus, who you are persecuting)

*"Meanwhile Saul was still breathing threats to slaughter the Lord's disciples. He went to the high priest and asked for letters addressed to the synagogues of Damascus, that would authorise him to arrest and take to Jerusalem any followers of the Way, men or women, that he might find. It happened that... suddenly a light from Heaven shone all around him. He fell to the ground and then he heard a voice saying, 'Saul, Saul, why are you persecuting me?' 'Who are you, Lord?' he asked, and the answer came, 'I am Jesus, who you are persecuting.'"*
(Ac 9:1-6).

Christ appeared quite a few times after rising from the dead, and for different reasons. In showing himself to Mary Magdalene and the women, he returned the love which had made them follow Jesus to Galilee. He appeared before Peter and his other disciples, when their hearts were full of remorse and shame for not being present at the crucifixion. The two disciples from Emmaus, who met him along the road to Jerusalem, were lost and bewildered, but had Christ in their hearts. And when he appeared to his apostles, they were full of fear and despair, though they still talked about him. Thomas, who is archetype of every person who needs certainties to believe, also saw him. And he appeared to Saul, a strict observer of the law, even though Saul hated Jesus and wanted to destroy him and his followers. Jesus appeared to Saul: the New Testament says this on various occasions (Ac 9:1-9; 22:1-11; 26:1-18;

and 1 Co 15:8). It is not, after all, that surprising. Saul did not have a neutral or indifferent attitude towards Jesus. He fought Jesus strongly, to the very end. And Jesus wanted to strike him. Little can be done against indifference, but a passionate unbeliever offers God an opportunity: the resurrected Christ confronted Saul and his resistance crumbled. Jesus showed himself to a man who was fighting against him, in the very moment when Saul was combating him: *"I am Jesus, who you are persecuting" (Ac 9:5).* This story is topical even now. Christ is present in the persecuted disciple, he talks and converts through him...Christ appears to Saul like the Messiah. He takes Saul in hand and transforms him, making him a vessel worthy of God. Saul's conversion is a kind of resurrection, in which the Lord's return is clearly felt. There is a resonance to Christ's words even today: *"If the world hates you, you must realise that it hated me before it hated you. If you belonged to the world, the world would love you as its own; but because you do not belong to this world... the world hates you... The time is coming when anyone who kills you will think he is doing a holy service to God" (Jn 15:18-19; 16:2).*

Why does the world hate Christ's disciple? Because he is open to the Word; he follows the light, while the world prefers the power of darkness. The disciple was chosen by Jesus to continue his mission of salvation, and the world of unbelievers does not accept Jesus, it fights against the Kingdom of God and hates anyone who brings the Word of Christ with him. The majestic figure of Jesus dominates this panel of the Holy Door, surrounded by rays of lights. He has overcome his persecutor, who has fallen to the ground.

# OPENING THE HOLY DOOR

## STO AD OSTIVM ET PVLSO (Look, I am standing at the door, knocking)

*"Look, I am standing at the door, knocking. If one of you hears me calling and opens the door, I will come in and share a meal at that person's side. Anyone who proves victorious I will allow to share my throne, just as I myself overcome and have taken my seat with my Father on his throne. Let anyone who can hear, listen to what the Spirit is saying to the churches"*
*(Rv 3:20-22).*

The last panel of the Holy Door shows the moment of its opening. On the morning of December 24 1949, Pope Pius XII drew close to the door, and knocked on it with a precious hammer made specially for this purpose. He thereby inaugurated the twenty-sixth Holy Year in history. During that year the world, which had strayed from God like the prodigal son, wasting all its riches, returned to its merciful Father, whose embrace is large enough to welcome everyone who turns to him.

Looking at the figure of Pius XII on the panel, one can hear the words he used in the bull inaugurating this Holy Year, "Iubileum maximum": *"We must have the same spirit of piety which in past centuries inspired the faithful to overcome every kind of difficulty, and come to Rome, often on foot, to cleanse their sins in tears of grief, imploring God's forgiveness and peace.*

This door is full of meanings, and they should be remembered in crossing its threshold. It stands for conversion, which is sincere when an inner change occurs in the person. Through conversion, we understand God's love for us, and willingly return to him, who so willingly forgives.

It stands for mercy. On the other side of this doorway, one can find a God who forgives. When a sinner returns to him, he starts the feast of rejoicing in Heaven.

It stands for justice or sanctity. The doorposts were marked with the blood of Christ, who was just. Everyone must enjoy its benefits: fervent believers will grow in justice and charity, fidelity and love of Christ and the Church. The half-hearted will be filled with enthusiasm, and those who have strayed will find their way home. The words engraved on the doors themselves are an invitation: *"Look, I am standing at the door, knocking. If one of you hears me calling and opens the door, I will come in and share a meal at that person's side"* (Rv 3:20).

God is a beggar, who begs for love, continually wandering around to pick up shreds of it.

Our home is not worthy to receive him, but he is worthy to enter it.

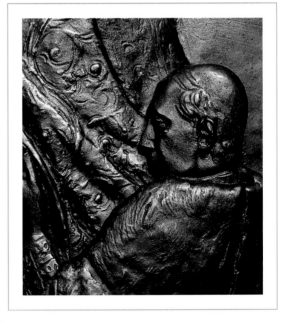

The Christian should be afraid of one thing. He should be afraid of not hearing God's knock, of not opening the door to him. A discreet guest does not insist. If no-one expects him and he is rejected, he moves on. This was St.Augustine's fear: *"I fear that Jesus may pass by, knock, and I not open to him. Will he be back a second time?"*.

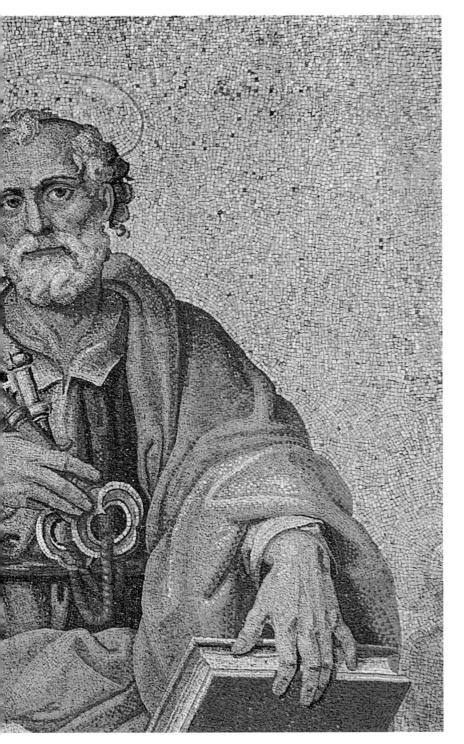

# The Holy Year Popes

*L*ife in the Church is moved by the Holy Spirit, of which Jesus said: "The Spirit is like the wind, that blows where it pleases; you can hear its sound, but you cannot tell where it comes from or where it is going" (see Jn 3:8). The Holy Spirit moves forces which visibly operate within the Church and also those which are hidden within it. It guides and moulds those who are gifted with sensitive spiritual antennae and are willing to be instruments of good within the Church.

The activities of these people, whether they belong to the church hierarchy or are simply part of the faithful, are not motivated by material gain or personal ambition. In a particular moment of their lives, God called them to work in his vineyard, and they answered him freely, without questioning his will.

The Jubilee is also an event in the Church provoked by the Holy Spirit. It takes place at a specific time, and fulfils a need of Christianity. The Church recognises this need, regulates its expression from the very beginning and provides rules to direct its future development.

*T*he Julibee originated from pilgrimages to holy places, particularly to Rome. Forgiveness of sins could be obtained at the tomb of St.Peter, under the guidance of his successors.

Throughout the centuries, and to this day, pilgrims feel that in Rome they touch the very heart of Christianity. Here they can experience the intrinsic qualities of their religion and the universality of their faith, professing it with people from different races and social conditions.

This has always happened in the history of Christian Rome! But in particular moments of time, such as the end of a millennium or the beginning of a century, the atmosphere clearly says that something new is about to happen, and that after the devastation of war, there is a need for peace among nations, in families, among individuals. And if humanity asks God for the forgiveness it needs, then this "new" something can be born.

*O*n the night of January 1 1300, the beginning of the civil year in Rome, a memorable event occurred: throngs of people crowded into St.Peter's. News had spread that on that day an indulgence could be obtained which pardoned men's sins, re-establishing their peace with God. The crowds astonished everyone, including Pope Boniface VIII.

The belief that a pilgrimage to St.Peter's during that year would completely eliminate the pilgrim's sins, was so strong that Boniface VIII ordered that research be done to find out if any such occurrence had been documented in the past. But nothing was found.

From January 1 onwards, this belief in the remission of sins increased and so did the number of pilgrims to the Basilica, both from Rome and from outside the city. On February 4, the crowds were particularly large, because traditionally on that day the Veil of Veronica, with Christ's image impressed on it, was shown to the faithful. Boniface VIII encouraged this spontaneous gathering of crowds, supporting their belief and ordering that the list of privileges to be obtained be drawn up and published from the ambo of the church on February 22, the feast day of the *cattedra Petri*.

With so many people flocking to Rome, a river of money apparently flooded the city.

There are stories of clerics who "raked up" coins thrown on St. Peter's tomb. Some said that all the coins were gold. Cardinal Stefaneschi, however, saw that they were "small coins of poor people". The offerings were used to restore the Basilica and for religious services.

The Holy Year of 1300 left a great impression on everyone. It was never forgotten, nor were the successive jubilees.

Events proved that attracting the faithful to Rome, "the holy city where the Great Peter's successors live", had a providential effect.

# BONIFACE VIII

Benedetto Gaetani, Pope Boniface VIII, was a man of high moral standards. He had a strong character, and stirred up opposition and denigration, even after his death. Boniface had a goal, the same goal of his predecessors, from Nicholas I (858-867) to Innocent III (1198-1216): papal supremacy in all the kingdoms of the world. The Jubilee he proclaimed was part of this design: it encouraged peace between the Christian nations so that papal supremacy could then be implemented. The Pope was a clever and shrewd man, who promoted goodness. Because of this, he did not stop the flow of pilgrims to Rome and responded positively to their requests for indulgences. Specifically, he responded with the bull "Privilegium", which begins with the words, *"Antiquorum habet fida relatio"*, meaning "There is a relationship worthy of the faith of the people of antiquity: that is, everyone who comes to Rome

1294-1303

and visits the venerable basilica dedicated to the principal apostle, will receive ample indulgence and remission of their sins". Anyone visiting the basilicas dedicated to the apostles Peter and Paul would receive complete pardon for their sins. Romans were obliged to make the visits for thirty consecutive days, while people from out of town were allowed fifteen days of visiting. Before this document was made public, it was left as an offering on the altar of St.Peter's, an extraordinary way of making the bull known. It was Boniface's gift, offered joyfully to the Basilica and to the Church throughout the ages. According to Cardinal Stefaneschi, the Pope "profoundly loved the Church of God".

Boniface had the text of the bull carved in marble, so that it can still be seen today, seven hundred years later, in the entrance to St.Peter's. A fresco in St.John Lateran, attributed to Giotto, gives us an image of what happened in St.Peter's on February 22, 1300. Cardinal Stefaneschi's account tells us that the Pope stood at the ambo of St.Peter's, covered in silk and cloth-of-gold, and proclaimed the indulgence. He was assisted by a bald priest in a lavish dalmatic, while an acolyte on the Pope's left read the oblong parchment containing the *"Privilegium"* bull. According to Giovanni Villani, a Florentine merchant turned chronicler for the Jubilee, the pilgrims that year included Cimabue, Giotto and the musician Casella. Villani does not, however, mention Dante. This great poet never himself wrote that he had received indulgence in 1300; but he did describe pilgrims going to St.Peter's and the countryside they moved through. Scholars who assert that Dante never took part in this Holy Year, explain the knowledge he shows of Jubilee events in the Divine Comedy and other minor works, as accounts referred by friends and acquaintances who had made the pilgrimage to Rome. Only once in his life did the poet Dante feel the need to imitate the many pilgrims who "go to see that blessed image, which Jesus Christ left us as a beautiful symbol of himself" (Vita nuova, XL; Parad., XXXI, 103).

| 1300 | 1st jubilee |
|------|-------------|
| 1350 | |
| 1390 | |
| 1400 | |
| 1423 | |
| 1450 | |
| 1475 | |
| 1500 | |
| 1525 | |
| 1550 | |
| 1575 | |
| 1600 | |
| 1625 | |
| 1650 | |
| 1675 | |
| 1700 | |
| 1725 | |
| 1750 | |
| 1775 | |
| 1825 | |
| 1875 | |
| 1900 | |
| 1925 | |
| 1950 | |
| 1975 | |
| 2000 | |

# CLEMENT VI

The 1350 Jubilee was celebrated when Pope Clement VI was out of Rome. He was in Avignon, along the Rhône, doing his best to claim the surrounding area for the Church. The city of Rome, abandoned at that time by the papacy, had fallen into economic, social and political decay. This is why ambassadors were repeatedly sent to Avignon by the notables of Rome, asking the pope to come back. A delegation sent in 1342 actually suggested to Clement the need to hold a jubilee in 1350. One of their arguments for this request was that the human beings rarely lived for one hundred years, and therefore the jubilee benefits could be extended to only a limited number of people.

One of the ambassadors on that occasion was the poet Francesco Petrarca. Cola di Rienzo was also part of the delegation, together with representatives from the three classes of Roman citizens: nobles, the middle classes, and

1342-1352

the populace. Cola di Rienzo's elegant oratorical style was much admired by the Pope.

On January 23 1343, Clement promulgated the bull *"Unigenitus Dei Filius"*, stating that the jubilee would be celebrated every fifty years from then onwards. There were two reasons for this decision: the lives of human beings were short, and in that span they had a great need for purification, remission of sins and spiritual reconciliation. Also, the Jewish jubilee recurred every fifty years.

This bull was the first official papal document to outline the doctrine of indulgences. It stated that the Church is depository of Christ's superabundant merits. These merits, together with those of the Virgin Mary and all the saints, form a kind of treasure.

The Holy Year focused on earning spiritual gifts. And at the time people reacted joyfully, for the Pope granted these spiritual gifts "for the benefit of the souls of the faithful". In order to earn the jubilee indulgence, the faithful had to visit the basilicas of St.Peter and St.Paul and that of the Holy Saviour and St.John at the Lateran. There were many pilgrims, including Francesco Petrarca. He was a profoundly spiritual man, with a great capacity for prayer and detachment from worldly things, and his eligibility for indulgence was increased by a long penitential stay in Viterbo: a horse had kicked him and broken Petrarca's leg, forcing immobility and reflection on the poet. Another pilgrim who inspired admiration in Rome during the 1350 Holy Year was Brigida of Sweden. She had come to Rome to make ready for the Pope's return, and stayed in the city for a quarter of a century. Her presence was significant and effective: she was full of mystical and purifying zeal and the light of her sanctity led the way for pilgrims.

Clement, however, did not return to Rome for the Jubilee. He sent two cardinals instead, and the faithful felt his lack. If he had come to Rome, the Pope could have given them a sense of direction in those confused times, since Clement was a cultivated man, a good speaker, full of charity and generosity.

# URBAN VI

The conclave had not been held in Rome for more than seventy-five years. In 1378, rioting went on during the conclave, with protesting Romans shouting at the cardinals, "we want him (the pope) to be Roman, or at least Italian." The archbishop of Bari, Bartolomeo Prignano, was elected, and he took the name of Urban VI.

Urban had considerable moral qualities. His goals as a pope were: to re-establish the papacy's complete autonomy, to re-introduce a strong and serious ecclesiastical discipline, and to re-organize the Curia.

Unfortunately, he lacked those qualities of urbanity, prudence, discretion and tact which are particularly necessary in difficult times.

Many people used this as a pretext to oppose Urban, and actually elected an antipope, Robert of Geneva, who installed himself in Avignon, and thus began the

1378-1389

Great Schism of the west (1378-1417).

Urban VI had proclaimed the 1390 Jubilee in April of 1389, to improve Roman society and religious life. On this occasion it was decided that jubilees would take place every thirty-three years, instead of every fifty years, in remembrance of Christ's lifespan.

Gregory XI (1370-1378) had established rules about visiting the basilicas, and Urban confirmed these rules. In honour of the Virgin's extraordinary role in Salvation, a visit to the basilica of S.Maria Maggiore was added on to the other three designated basilicas, (St. Peter's, St. Paul's, St. John Lateran) in the bull *"Salvator noster Dominus"* (April 21, 1373).

Urban VI did not live long enough to see the beginning of the jubilee; in fact, he died on October 15, 1389.

Unfortunately, we do not have a complete version of Urban's indiction bull for the Holy Year, *"Salvator noster Dominus"*. It's essential parts are known to us through essays and publications, the parts where the Pope explains his reasons for reducing the time between jubilees: the shortness of human life (many people never even reached fifty), and underscoring the length of Christ's own lifespan, imprinting the memory of what he had done to save the world.

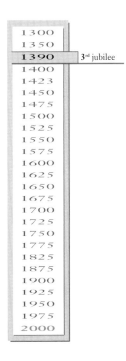

| | |
|---|---|
| 1300 | |
| 1350 | |
| **1390** | 3rd jubilee |
| 1400 | |
| 1423 | |
| 1450 | |
| 1475 | |
| 1500 | |
| 1525 | |
| 1550 | |
| 1575 | |
| 1600 | |
| 1625 | |
| 1650 | |
| 1675 | |
| 1700 | |
| 1725 | |
| 1750 | |
| 1775 | |
| 1825 | |
| 1875 | |
| 1900 | |
| 1925 | |
| 1950 | |
| 1975 | |
| 2000 | |

# BONIFACE IX

Urban VI
died before of
the Holy Year he
had proclaimed began.
His successor, the Neapolitan
Pietro Tomacelli, welcomed the pilgrims benevolently.
They came from all the nations professing obedience
to the Roman pope, and wanted to receive the indulgences proclaimed for 1390. There must not have
been very many pilgrims; a lot of people were dis-
gusted by the spectacle of a warring, split Church,
with two popes, two observances, and a double spiritual heritage. Much of the faithful also found the novelty of the thirty-three year jubilee strange and unfa-
miliar.
The pilgrim's most memorable impression was meet-
ing Pope Boniface XI. He was only thirty-six at the
time of his election, and had a gentle, welcoming
manner. He was a prudent man, who led a pure life.
During his pontificate, Boniface was able to strength-

1389-1404

en papal authority. Ten years after the 1390 Jubilee, in the year 1400, the conviction that it was more appropriate to celebrate the Holy Year as a centenary, at the beginning of each century, re-emerged.

Crowds of pilgrims therefore set out for Rome. They swelled like rivers, causing quite a few problems for the civil authorities.

These pilgrims were called "Bianchi" (literally "Whites") because of the white hoods they wore, with a red cross on top. Since they habitually whipped themselves to instill self-discipline, they were also called "Flagellants" ("Flagellanti" or "Battuti").

They were received in St.Peter's by the Pope, and were shown the Veil of Veronica. Boniface was moved by the pilgrim's great faith and piety and granted them the jubilee forgiveness. Boniface IX did not proclaim this Holy Year with the usual indiction bull, but he was definitely the heart of the celebration. The peoples' hope of receiving the jubilee in the moment of passage from one century to the next was once again fulfilled.

During the Jubilee of 1400, German pilgrims were assisted for the first time by an organization from their own country. This charitable organization was founded in the hospice of S.Maria dell'Anima. Even a graveyard was created for them in the entrance to the Vatican, so that German pilgrims buried there could rest in an oasis of peace.

Until just a few years ago, a mosaic portaying Charlemagne could be seen on the outside of a building in the graveyard. The inscription read, "A nest of swallows on the path of St.Peter's basilica. A German house (dwelling) in Golden Rome".

| | |
|---|---|
| 1300 | |
| 1350 | |
| 1390 | |
| **1400** | 4th jubilee |
| 1423 | |
| 1450 | |
| 1475 | |
| 1500 | |
| 1525 | |
| 1550 | |
| 1575 | |
| 1600 | |
| 1625 | |
| 1650 | |
| 1675 | |
| 1700 | |
| 1725 | |
| 1750 | |
| 1775 | |
| 1825 | |
| 1875 | |
| 1900 | |
| 1925 | |
| 1950 | |
| 1975 | |
| 2000 | |

# MARTIN V

After the
Great Schism
of the west (dur-
ing which the Church
had three popes), Cardinal
Ottone Colonna was elected, taking the name of Martin
V. His election occurred on the feast of St.Martin, November 11, 1417, in Constance, Germany. He was the
legitimate pope: the Church was once more united. Martin V was simple and modest, a worthy man with a dis-
tinguished and friendly manner. A peaceful and joyous
atmosphere prevailed. Little wonder, then, that Martin
was called "*Temporum suorum felicitas*", a title which can
still be seen on his tomb in St.John Lateran.
Unfortunately, when Martin V first arrived in Rome
from Constance, the city was even physically in a disas-
trous state.
There were doors and windows missing in the Vatican after Gregory XI's restoration. The roof of St.Peter's was in
poor condition. St.John Lateran was a ruin. The Pope

1417-1431

stepped in at this point, beginning a whole restoration process which reached its zenith of Renaissance magnificence under Nicholas V and Sixtus IV. Martin also reformed the papal Curia, giving it an international character. He took an interest in disciplining the clergy, restored religious congregations and nominated such valid cardinals as Domenico Capranica and Nicolò Cesarini. He re-conquered lands which the Church had lost (Braccio da Montone) and proclaimed to all the great powers of the time that Rome alone was the centre of the papacy. He summoned artists to work there. Gentile da Fabriano frescoed the nave of St.John Lateran, and Masaccio painted the story of the basilica's foundation in S.Maria Maggiore, portraying Martin V as Pope Liberius.

To demonstrate his authority, Pope Martin revived Urban VI's idea about the Holy Year celebration, and thirty-three years after the 1390 Jubilee he proclaimed a new one. A bull of Paul II bears witness to this fact.

Just as had occurred in 1400, there was no indiction bull for this jubilee. It seems, however, that for the first time in history a door was opened for the occasion in St.John Lateran, called the "golden" or holy door.

This information was given by a chronicler from Viterbo and by a Florentine, Giovanni Rucellai, in his notes on the jubilee.

Bernardino da Siena was one of the preachers who prepared people for the Holy Year. Enea Silvio Piccolomini wrote that "All Rome would gather to hear his sermons, and often cardinals would be among the public and sometimes even the Pope". The presence in Rome at that time of Francesca Romana dei Ponziani, a noblewoman who had turned her palace in Trastevere into a centre for charitable work and assistance, should also be noted. Martin V had a good number of German pilgrims come to Rome that year. Humanists were not overly pleased about this. Poggio Bracciolini described these pilgrims as "an inundation of barbarians who covered the city with filth".

The Renaissance began after this jubilee.

| 1300 | |
| 1350 | |
| 1390 | |
| 1400 | |
| **1423** | 5th jubilee |
| 1450 | |
| 1475 | |
| 1500 | |
| 1525 | |
| 1550 | |
| 1575 | |
| 1600 | |
| 1625 | |
| 1650 | |
| 1675 | |
| 1700 | |
| 1725 | |
| 1750 | |
| 1775 | |
| 1825 | |
| 1875 | |
| 1900 | |
| 1925 | |
| 1950 | |
| 1975 | |
| 2000 | |

# NICHOLAS V

Tommaso Parentucelli became a cardinal only two months before he was elected pope. His election was unanimous and joyful. The new pope had exceptional qualities both of heart and mind. Physically he was "a man of small stature, and of simple birth". He did not even have a coat-of-arms and so he adopted the decussed keys when he became pope. A German contemporary of Nicholas' commented that in Germany he would never have become even a canon. Yet chroniclers such as Vespasiano da Bisticci thought highly of the new Pope, considering him a virtuous, sincere, modest and hard-working man, with a welcoming and benign nature, a man of peace "who during his pontificate would use no other weapon than the Cross, given to him by Christ for self-defence". He was a cultivated man, who spent what little he possessed "on books and building". It was said that with Nicholas V, the Renaissance had been elected to

1447-1455

the throne of Peter. He never forgot his humanist friends, and the arts flourished again under his patronage. The jubilee was an important part of Nicholas' program for peace and universal reinstatement. He formally proclaimed the next Holy Year on January 29, 1449; it was to begin on the following Christmas. In his bull, *"Immensa et innumerabilia"*, Nicholas outlined the steps to take both in preparing for and participating in the jubilee. He reminded the faithful of the "immense and countless favours of God's mercy, which God had entrusted to Peter and his successors, so that the faithful might find an easier entrance to the kingdom of heaven".

Special periods of time, when God's mercy flowed like a river among the peoples of the earth, were to be counted among heaven's gifts, Nicholas added. They were the mystery of jubilee, offered to the faithful by their pope at specific times. The Pope was a source of inspiration for everyone who came to Rome for the Holy Year: this fragile, weak man walked barefoot through the city streets, visiting the basilicas. He ordered that the image of Christ be exposed every Sunday in St.Peter's, and that every Saturday the heads of Peter and Paul be shown in St.John Lateran. He also ordered that all the churches in Rome display their relics. Antonino da Firenzo described this as a "Golden Year". The faithful came from everywhere, and it was generally thought that they were more numerous than in previous years. During the Jubilee, on the feast of Pentecost, Nicholas canonised Bernardino da Siena, whom he had personally met and heard preach.

Four future saints came to Rome for the occasion: Giacomo della Marca, Giovanni da Capistrano, Pietro Regalato and Diego of Alcalà. St.Catherine of Bologna and Rita da Cascia were among the women pilgrims that year. Kings and princes also made the pilgrimage. Vespasiano da Bisticci wrote about the faithful, "They looked like ants in the streets of Rome and Florence...". As Enea Silvio Piccolomini wrote:"Once the splendour of imperial dignity eclipsed everything. Now the Pope's splendour is much greater". It was always to be so thereafter!

| |
|---|
| 1300 |
| 1350 |
| 1390 |
| 1400 |
| 1423 |
| **1450**  6th jubilee |
| 1475 |
| 1500 |
| 1525 |
| 1550 |
| 1575 |
| 1600 |
| 1625 |
| 1650 |
| 1675 |
| 1700 |
| 1725 |
| 1750 |
| 1775 |
| 1825 |
| 1875 |
| 1900 |
| 1925 |
| 1950 |
| 1975 |
| 2000 |

# SIXTUS IV

After Paul II died at the age of fifty-three, a Franciscan, Cardinal Francesco Della Rovere, was elected. He was from the Ligurian town of Savona.

1471-1484

Sixtus IV was a great theologian; as a teacher he had given proof of profound learning; and the scholars of his time held the future pope in high esteem as a controversialist. He loved culture, and enlarged the Vatican Library. He also invested his energies in decorating the streets of Rome; he put the roads in working order, and renovated the Hospital of S.Spirito and some of Rome's churches.

He also dedicated two Renaissance churches "ex novo" to the Virgin Mary: S.Maria del Popolo and S.Maria della Pace. He had the Sistine Chapel built in the Vatican, dedicating it to the Virgin; and he fixed the Ponte Rotto ("Broken Bridge") for the 1475 Holy Year, re-building it in travertine. Because of all the work Sixtus had done in Rome, increasing the city's beauty, he was known as "Urbis restaurator".

Sixtus IV's jubilee was the seventh Holy Year. It had been proclaimed by Paul II with the bull *"Ineffabilis Providentia"* on April 19, 1470.

This bull definitively established the frequency of jubilees, eliminating the contradictory orders of previous popes such as Clement VI (every fifty years) and Urban VI (every thirty-three years).

After summing up the criteria previously used to determine their frequency, Paul II ordered that jubilees be once more held every twenty-five years.

His reason was the shortness of human life, caused by public calamities, which in turn were provoked by sinfulness.

At the same time, Paul II decided that all Holy Years would henceforth begin and end on the night before Christmas.

Had Paul II not died beforehand, he would have been the first pope to apply these rules.

His successor, Sixtus IV, ratified Paul's decision about the twenty-five year frequency in a bull, *"Salvator noster Dei Filius"*, published on March 26, 1472. To this he added an important detail in the bull *"Quemadmodum operosi"* on August 26, 1473: all other types of indulgence were suspended. This would increase the Jubilee's prestige, since the faithful coming to Rome would thereby acquire exceptional abundance of grace.

Unfortunately, there were not many pilgrims that year. To complicate matters, the Tiber river flooded, causing endless illnesses.

Several events characterised the 1475 Holy Year. Printing had just been invented in 1444, and Sixtus used it to proclaim the jubilee and organise it. And there was another novelty as well: for the first time in history the jubilee, thereafter recurring every twenty-five years, was called the "Holy Year".

| | |
|---|---|
| 1300 | |
| 1350 | |
| 1390 | |
| 1400 | |
| 1423 | |
| 1450 | |
| **1475** | 7th jubilee |
| 1500 | |
| 1525 | |
| 1550 | |
| 1575 | |
| 1600 | |
| 1625 | |
| 1650 | |
| 1675 | |
| 1700 | |
| 1725 | |
| 1750 | |
| 1775 | |
| 1825 | |
| 1875 | |
| 1900 | |
| 1925 | |
| 1950 | |
| 1975 | |
| 2000 | |

# ALEXANDER VI

Chronologically speaking, the last years of the 15th century and the first years of the 16th century mark the end of the Middle Ages and the beginning of the modern era. They were characterised by confusion and moral jolts. The pope of that period, unfortunately, was unable to bring light to his time or to check the great upheaval of mankind and events. "The name of Alexander VI will sadly go down in history as the equivalent of baseness and wickedness".
Yet at the end of the century, this man proclaimed the new Holy Year with a truly religious spirit, which in him was unexpected. He wanted the Holy Year to have a particularly imposing character. A master of ceremonies, chosen specially for the occasion, was to coordinate the beginning, performance and end of the Holy Year events. The jubilee ceremony rules used even today go back to Alexander VI, with just a few

1492-1503

changes. He decided that holy doors should be opened not just in St.John Lateran, but also in the other basilicas: St.Peter's, St.Paul's and S.Maria Maggiore.

This is how things went in St.Peter's.

On the extreme right of the façade of old St.Peter's (the Constantinian basilica), there was a small door, possibly a service door. The Pope had it transformed and turned into the Holy Door.

This decision led to the destruction of a chapel inside the basilica, which John VII has built in honour of the Virgin Mary. Its precious mosaics were lost, and the beautiful dedicatory image of the Madonna portrayed as a queen ended up, somewhat mysteriously, in Florence, in the Servite church.

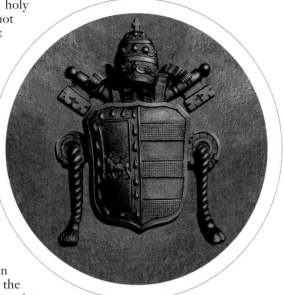

During the first Christmas Vespers in 1499, Alexander VI was carried in his gestatorial chair to St.Peter's Holy Door. Surrounded by singing and prayers, he knocked on it three times.

The Holy Door collapsed, and after the Pope had knelt in prayer, he crossed the threshold of great forgiveness. The same ceremony was performed in opening the doors of the other basilicas.

Throughout that year, Alexander presided over all the ceremonies celebrated in Rome for the occasion. It was a period when the spirit of the Jubilee seemed to triumph.

Alexander VI published quite a few bulls regarding the Jubilee of 1500.

The first of them, *"Consueverunt Romani Pontifices"*, mentioned by Burckhardt in his diary, outlines the Pope's ideas about getting ready for the jubilee: for him, it was essential to be spiritually prepared for this great event. All other indulgences were suspended.

Another bull, *"Inter curas multiplices"*, described how to open the Holy Door. Anyone making a donation towards building the new St.Peter's, would be granted a special indulgence, applicable to the souls of the dead. Every one of these bulls urged the faithful to make the most of that year of grace!

| |
|---|
| 1300 |
| 1350 |
| 1390 |
| 1400 |
| 1423 |
| 1450 |
| 1475 |
| **1500** 8th jubilee |
| 1525 |
| 1550 |
| 1575 |
| 1600 |
| 1625 |
| 1650 |
| 1675 |
| 1700 |
| 1725 |
| 1750 |
| 1775 |
| 1825 |
| 1875 |
| 1900 |
| 1925 |
| 1950 |
| 1975 |
| 2000 |

# CLEMENT VII

Serious and tempestuous events were building up during the pontificate of Clement VII (Giuliano de' Medici), and they conditioned it by noticeably reducing its spiritual impact. These events were: the "reforms" of Luther, Zwingli and Calvin, which separated the Germanic countries from Rome; the English schism caused by Henry VIII; and the war between Charles V and Francis I, which was fought in Italian territory (see the Battle of Pavia in 1525, ending with Francis I's imprisonment at the Certosa of Pavia).

There was little that Clement VII could do to keep the consequences of these overpowering events under control. Perhaps he lacked the strength of character to stop the war and to reconcile the two kings. This war was the first political rupture in Europe at that time.

As to the religious contrasts, Clement and his court apparently underestimated the danger of the reformist

1523-1534

movement. They believed that it resembled other temporary ruptures within the Church itself, and in time would die out, like many monkish feuds had in the past.

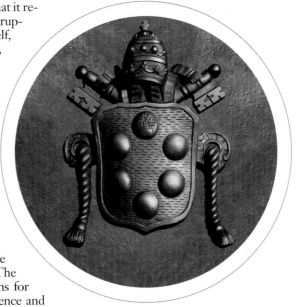

Clement proclaimed the Holy Year for 1525, following Paul II's prescription for a jubilee every twenty-five years. The Pope ordered that the publication of the indiction bull be particularly solemn, and he personally opened the Holy Door in St.Peter's, delegating cardinals to perform the ceremony in the other patriarchal basilicas. The bull described the conditions for receiving the jubilee indulgence and what conditions had to be met by people who could not physically come to Rome. Finally, Clement granted that the indulgence could be used for the souls of the dead.

The latter provision caused a crude anti-Roman dispute. Friars preaching about the indulgence would ask the faithful for alms, and this gave rise to the phrase "when the gold falls in the money-box, the soul leaps out of Purgatory".

The painful consequence of this was that fewer pilgrims came to Rome, particularly from the German countries. Publications actually circulated in these countries, which ironically compared the Pope's jubilee with the jubilee of Christ. This spirit re-emerged during the Sack of Rome in 1527, when the invading German soldiers would parody the papal ceremonies and indulgences.

Gaetano Thiene was in Rome for the 1525 Holy Year. The example of his charity later produced organisations to help the needy, while his qualities as a priest inspired new orders of clerics, a concrete answer to the Protestant revolution.

A memorable event of 1525 was that for the first time a coin was minted to commemorate the Holy Year. The Nativity in Bethlehem was on the front of the coin, to remind people that the Holy Year began at Christmas. On the back, a pope was seen opening the Holy Door, with St. Peter rising above him and indicating the unlocked gates of Heaven. The inscription explained the scene's meaning: "And the celestial doors are opened".

| |
|---|
| 1300 |
| 1350 |
| 1390 |
| 1400 |
| 1423 |
| 1450 |
| 1475 |
| 1500 |
| **1525**     9th jubilee |
| 1550 |
| 1575 |
| 1600 |
| 1625 |
| 1650 |
| 1675 |
| 1700 |
| 1725 |
| 1750 |
| 1775 |
| 1825 |
| 1875 |
| 1900 |
| 1925 |
| 1950 |
| 1975 |
| 2000 |

# JULIUS III

Towards the end of 1549, Paul III (Alessandro Farnese) decided to proclaim the tenth Holy Year in 1550. But he was prevented from doing so by his sudden death on November 10, 1549. Paul's successor, Julius III, Giovanni Maria Ciocchi del Monte, was elected and installed in February 1550. Just two days after his incoronation as pope, on February 24, Julius proclaimed and opened the Holy Year with the bull *"Si pastores ovium"*, following the guidelines of past documents. Del Monte had been one of Paul III's legates at the Council of Trent. After he was elected pope, he dedicated much of his time to supporting and regulating the Council's results, in spite of Charles V's opposition and the interference of princes and kings. Julius inherited Paul III's intentions, and without wasting any time, he proclaimed the jubilee and himself ceremoniously opened the Holy Door in St.Peter's. The formal grandeur of the opening ceremony was sub-

1550-1555

sequently adopted by the diplomatic missions and legations of all the countries who came to Rome to pay tribute to the new pope and to make the jubilee visits. Their processions were very ostentatious, for though they were supposed to have a penitential character, they were actually displays of power and worldliness. Even the Marquis Francisco de Borja, who had come to Rome to receive forgiveness for his sins, was accompanied by thirty gorgeous and elegant cavaliers. In opposition to this spirit, the Confraternity of the Holy Trinity began its evangelical work at that time, without any outward show or ostentation. It's looked after pilgrims, fraternally welcoming anyone who came to Rome without any distinction of their nationality, unlike the pre-existing hospices connected with the national churches. During this Jubilee, which was extended to the Epiphany of 1551 to compensate for the delay in the beginning, the Confraternity offered hospitality and looked after about 70,000 pilgrims, often assisting as many as six-hundred people a day. This pious work was inspired by Philip Neri, who was just starting his activities in Rome, and was a manifestation of the Roman church's charity. The Confraternity received high praise: perfect service, excellent food, abundant soups, meat, tuna or herring, a loaf of bread, a jug of wine, fresh sheets. The Confraternities work was a concrete way of opposing the reformers, who were disrupting the Church in Germany, England, and the areas of Europe around the Danube and the Mediterranean, which the Turks were besieging. The spirit of conquest was also a form of opposition: new Christians were being converted by missionaries in the Americas and in India, taking the place of those who had left the Church of Rome. During this period, there was literally a flowering of new saints, who came to revive the Church, spreading moral and spiritual values everywhere and creating an atmosphere of Catholic renewal. Among the lay people present at the Jubilee, the old, sick Michelangelo visited the prescribed churches on horseback, receiving a "double" indulgence. He actually had the Pope's permission to do so!

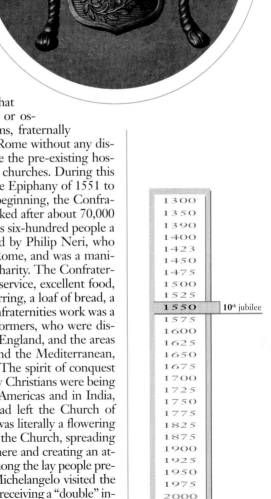

| | |
|---|---|
| 1300 | |
| 1350 | |
| 1390 | |
| 1400 | |
| 1423 | |
| 1450 | |
| 1475 | |
| 1500 | |
| 1525 | |
| **1550** | 10th jubilee |
| 1575 | |
| 1600 | |
| 1625 | |
| 1650 | |
| 1675 | |
| 1700 | |
| 1725 | |
| 1750 | |
| 1775 | |
| 1825 | |
| 1875 | |
| 1900 | |
| 1925 | |
| 1950 | |
| 1975 | |
| 2000 | |

# GREGORY XIII

The fourth
Holy Year of
the 16th century,
held in 1575, was one of
the most exemplary ones ever cel-
ebrated. It coincided with the conference of Catholic renewal, which had resumed after the Council of Trent,
with Gregory XIII playing an important role, together
with two other popes: Pius V (1566-1572) and Sixtus V
(1585-1590). Gregory proclaimed the Holy Year on the
feast of the Ascension in 1574, first with the bull *"Dominus ac Redemptor"*, and then with another Advent bull
during the same year. This is an indication of how
scrupulously Gregory wanted the jubilee to be organised.
After describing the Jubilee as a "healthy and pious insti-
tution" in the *"Dominus ac Redemptor"* bull, the Pope
urged the faithful to consider the vanity of earthly pos-
sessions, the shortness of life and the immense joy provided by the life of the spirit. During a secret consistory
held in November of that year, the Pope once again ex-

1572-1585

horted the cardinals to prepare themselves for the Holy Year and be an example to everyone, particularly pilgrims coming from over the Alps, of the spiritual riches available in Rome. The Holy Year was to be a sign of the revival of a truly Christian spirit among the faithful. Every worldly amusement was to be set aside, and for this reason the Pope forbid Carnival that year. Even though it was by then less showy than in the past, the celebration of Carnival would not have fitted in with the atmosphere of austerity and penance of this Jubilee. The Pope set an example of this spirit for the clergy by personally visiting the four basilicas to receive indulgence. On those occasions, his following included cardinals and prelates; among them was Carlo Borromeo. Gregory XIII's Holy Year had a missionary character, and the conversion of non-believers and heretics were much discussed topics. English Catholics, who at that time were being persecuted, also had the possibility of receiving the jubilee indulgence. Their penance was to recite 15 rosaries. There were many pilgrims that year, welcomed by the confraternities, whose manifestations of faith and piety in the basilicas and at the tombs of the martyrs were quite lively. The members of the Confraternity of the Holy Trinity were particularly notable on these occasions for their generosity and organisational capacities. From an architectural point of view, Rome presented an encouraging spectacle to the pilgrims. The Mediaeval city had been turned upside down by new building projects. Pope Gregory restored many churches, ordering the rectors to give these churches the decorum required for the House of God. He consecrated the church of the Gesù (the foundation stone had been laid in June, 1558), and was pleased to see it opened to public worship. The religious face of the city was changing. Mediaeval Rome with its bell-towers was being transformed into a Renaissance city of domes. Michelangelo's towering dome of St.Peter's rose above all the other domes in Rome. The pilgrims could see it from far away, overshadowing the façade of the old Constantinian basilica.

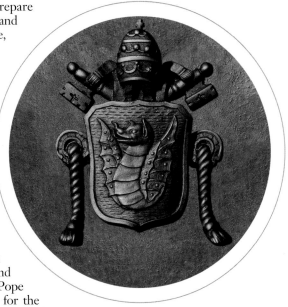

| 1300 | |
| 1350 | |
| 1390 | |
| 1400 | |
| 1423 | |
| 1450 | |
| 1475 | |
| 1500 | |
| 1525 | |
| 1550 | |
| **1575** | 11th jubilee |
| 1600 | |
| 1625 | |
| 1650 | |
| 1675 | |
| 1700 | |
| 1725 | |
| 1750 | |
| 1775 | |
| 1825 | |
| 1875 | |
| 1900 | |
| 1925 | |
| 1950 | |
| 1975 | |
| 2000 | |

# CLEMENT VIII

Clement VIII, who was born Ippolito Aldobrandini and became pope in 1592, called a new Jubilee on May 19, 1599, by publishing the bull "*Annus Domini placabilis*". This bull described the traditions of the "centenary year", which was to be "celebrated in Rome, not with vain and pagan superstition, but with religious ceremonies and a great gathering of Christians", as had already been established by Boniface VIII in an apostolic decree. Clement VIII's bull also dealt with changes in the Church after the religious defections of those years, and invited everyone who had left the Church to return to it. Their return to the fold would be facilitated by the overall climate of repentance.

On October 30, 1599, as the beginning of the Jubilee drew near, Clement VIII sent a letter, "*Tempus acceptabile*", to each bishop, urging them to come to Rome and be a good example for the faithful in their dioceses.

1592-1605

Clement personally set the tone of piety and spirituality for the Jubilee. He visited the four Jubilee basilicas devotedly. And on his way back, the Pope would visit the Arciconfraternita della SS.ma Trinità (Confraternity of the Holy Trinity), where the memory of St.Philip Neri was still very much alive, and would humbly wash pilgrim's feet and serve them at table. In spite of the numerous maladies afflicting him, which were serious enough to make it necessary to postpone the Holy Door opening ceremony to December 31, Clement performed all the penitential rituals necessary to obtain the indulgences. During Holy Week, he also substituted the Grand Penitentiary in St.Peter's, hearing confessions for hours on end.

As contemporary diarist wrote, "His Holiness wants to set an excellent example for the world". And everyone followed his example: nobles and common people, Christians and non-Christians, and even the Jews, "who usually made offerings for the pilgrims".

The Holy Year of 1600 was rendered memorable by the presence of this man, who was so gentle, intelligent and modest. He was particularly active in charity towards pilgrims and even paid for their lodgings out of the offerings which were destined for him. Bishops, prelates and priests were usually hosted for ten days at the Pope's expense.

An immense number of pilgrims came to Rome for this Holy Year. They were assisted by the various confraternities, who would not only materially organise the pilgrimages, but would also teach the pilgrims hymns, singing along with them during the processions to the patriarchal basilicas. These processions were likewise organised by the confraternities, who participated in them wearing their colourful habits and symbolic emblems.

Two saintly men were among the pilgrims, and their presence was strongly felt: Camillo de Lellis, who was so charitable to the sick, and Robert Bellarmino, succouring the victims of religious confusion.

| |
|---|
| 1300 |
| 1350 |
| 1390 |
| 1400 |
| 1423 |
| 1450 |
| 1475 |
| 1500 |
| 1525 |
| 1550 |
| 1575 |
| **1600**  12th jubilee |
| 1625 |
| 1650 |
| 1675 |
| 1700 |
| 1725 |
| 1750 |
| 1775 |
| 1825 |
| 1875 |
| 1900 |
| 1925 |
| 1950 |
| 1975 |
| 2000 |

# URBAN VIII

The thir-
teenth Jubilee
fell in 1625, at the
beginning of Urban VI-
II's pontificate. The Pope, born
Matteo Barberini, was elected in 1623.

1623-1644

The Holy Year was called with a bull, "*Omnes gentes plau-dite manibus*" on April 29, 1624. In this bull, Urban asked his bishops to spread instructions on how to obtain in-dulgences, and urged the great noblemen of the time to do charitable works and look after the material needs of pilgrims.

On December 24, 1624, he opened the Holy Door in St.Peter's Basilica. Prince Ladislaw of Poland was present at the ceremony; shortly afterwards, he became a canon of St.Peter's, so that he could touch the relics of Christ's image and the Holy Spear, and show them to the popu-lace.

In another important bull, dated January 30, 1625, Urban VIII made S.Maria in Trastevere the basilica for jubilee visits, instead of St.Paul's Outside the Walls. At that time the area around St.Paul's was thought to be plague-infested. Another problem for pilgrimages was the ongoing war between Genoa and Milan. Anyone who visited the basilicas in Rome and prayed for peace would receive indulgences, according to the bull *"Divinae misericordiae foribus"*, published on April 21, 1625. Immense numbers of pilgrims came to Rome, which at that time had a strongly Baroque culture. Instead of being religious acts, the pilgrimages turned into performances. Religious ceremonies were fleshed out and became exaggerated. Places of worship were heavily ornamented by ephemeral Baroque decorations. Movable props turned churches into stage sets, so that their religious significance was lost. Confraternities behaved particularly badly, with frequent rivalries and squabbling over their rights of precedence.

Fortunately, the Pope set a good example of piety. He went on foot to the Jubilee basilicas and assisted visiting pilgrims in the Trinity Hospice. Diary impressions written by pilgrims at that time were positive. The Benedictine abbot of St.Paul's in Carinzia wrote that, "We were particularly struck by the piety of foreigners...For my part, I saw nothing scandalous in Rome, but on the contrary a great deal of religious devotion".

Pope Urban not only made repeated visits to the churches prescribed for jubilee indulgences, he also listened to confessions in St.Peter's on numerous occasions, particularly on Holy Saturday, when he practised this sacrament for hours on end. Twelve pilgrims were given hospitality in the Vatican every day, and the Pope gave alms lavishly. He had the happy thought of sharing the Holy Year's spiritual effects with people who were materially unable to come to Rome and visit the tombs of the Apostles. These included cloistered orders, anchorites, hermits, the sick and people in jail; they were provided for in the papal letter *"Pontificia sollicitudo"* (January 29, 1625). During this Holy Year, the Pope canonised the Capuchin friar Felice da Cantalice.

|  | |
|---|---|
| 1300 | |
| 1350 | |
| 1390 | |
| 1400 | |
| 1423 | |
| 1450 | |
| 1475 | |
| 1500 | |
| 1525 | |
| 1550 | |
| 1575 | |
| 1600 | |
| **1625** | 13th jubilee |
| 1650 | |
| 1675 | |
| 1700 | |
| 1725 | |
| 1750 | |
| 1775 | |
| 1825 | |
| 1875 | |
| 1900 | |
| 1925 | |
| 1950 | |
| 1975 | |
| 2000 | |

Giovanni Battista Pamphilj, Pope Innocent X, was elected in 1644. Though he was already seventy years old, he took on his new responsibilities with a youthful vigour, partly owing to his robust health. His initiatives as pope include the fourteenth Jubilee, which he proclaimed with the bull "*Appropinquat, dilectissimi filii*" on May 4, 1649. In this bull, after paying formal homage to Rome as the capital city of sanctity and the place where the apostles' remains are kept, the Pope noted that the world was no longer as pious as it had been in ancient times. Many countries no longer practised Catholicism, and heresy kept them from rejoicing in the Jubilee and sharing in Heaven's blessings.

Innocent was deeply involved in preparations for the Holy Year, which was to be particularly grand, and did not allow himself to be distracted by his many other concerns. He was personally involved in its organisation and

**1644-1655**

also let his family participate: his sister-in-law, Olimpia Maidalchini, an imperious and ambitious woman, had an important role in the preparations. She had a strong will, and was thought to exert undue influence over the Pope. She completely took over the organisation of assistance to pilgrims. The effect of her influence was noticeable from even before the Jubilee began: in December, 1649 she invited all the noblewomen of the Roman court to hear a sermon preached by a Jesuit, and after the sermon Donna Olimpia herself spoke to the congregation, asking them for their co-operation.

Needless to say, all the ladies present were more than willing to help her. Donna Olimpia was not easily discouraged from pursuing her goals. For example, when the holy doors of the four main Roman basilicas had to be opened, she managed to have the door of Santa Maria Maggiore opened by her nephew, Francesco Maidalchini, instead of by the church's archpriest. This nephew was only seventeen and hadn't been ordained yet, but in spite of this Donna Olimpia had him nominated cardinal.

The Jubilee began, and the pilgrims started arriving. Most of them were drawn by the promise of God's forgiveness, which the pope could impart in Christ's name. The confraternities helped with both pilgrims and organisation, but very much in the spirit of the times. Processions including them were showy, fashionable events and religious ceremonies often degenerated into fights over precedence.

The Pope insisted that pilgrims had to meet the rigorous standard of thirty visits to the four basilicas, though some people noted that Innocent himself made the visits no more than fourteen or fifteen times. However, it should be noted that the Pope's health had seriously deteriorated, and by then he was quite frail.

This Holy Year is memorable to art historians, because St.John Lateran was completely transformed for the occasion by Francesco Borromini, who achieved a Baroque space out of the original paleo-Christian basilica.

| |
|---|
| 1300 |
| 1350 |
| 1390 |
| 1400 |
| 1423 |
| 1450 |
| 1475 |
| 1500 |
| 1525 |
| 1550 |
| 1575 |
| 1600 |
| 1625 |
| **1650**  14th jubilee |
| 1675 |
| 1700 |
| 1725 |
| 1750 |
| 1775 |
| 1825 |
| 1875 |
| 1900 |
| 1925 |
| 1950 |
| 1975 |
| 2000 |

# CLEMENT X

When Car-
dinal Emilio
Altieri was elected
pope he was eighty
years old, and part of his reluc-
tance to accept the nomination was due to his age. He
took the name of Clement in honour of Clement IX, his
predecessor. They both had gentle, pious natures and
years of experience in the Church's affairs. This experience proved useful when King Louis XIV obstinately
boycotted the Church's efforts to establish peace between
France, Spain and Holland.

1670-1676

Clement X supported Captain Sobieski against the
Turks. But he also concentrated his energies on organis-
ing and celebrating the Holy Year with great pomp.
 It had been solemnly proclaimed on April 16, 1674, with
the bull *"Ad Apostolicae vocis oraculum"*, which urged the
faithful to gather joyfully in Rome. There were good reasons for many pilgrims to come. Clement's optimistic
and hopeful invitation had a good effect: vast crowds of

pilgrims arrived, and were graciously welcomed by the confraternities, particularly by the Confraternity of the Holy Cross in the church of S.Marcello and the Confraternity of the Holy Trinity, who emulated St.Philip Neri in their mission of charity.

One of the pilgrims was Queen Christina of Sweden. She had converted to Catholicism, given up her throne, and was then welcomed in Rome by Pope Alexander VII as the living symbol of a triumphant Catholic Church, in a moment of political of insults and religious defeats. Christina was present at all the Jubilee celebrations; at the opening ceremony of the Holy Door, she audibly scolded a Protestant guest, who had not knelt when the wall fell down. She would personally meet every important pilgrimage. And pilgrims were usually eager to see her and speak to her, not so much because she was a very cultivated woman, but because of her great sacrifice, which brought honour and prestige to the Roman Catholic church.

In spite of his age, the Pope visited both the Jubilee basilicas and sick pilgrims in hospices. He wanted Rome to be more obviously Christian and so he had the Cardinal Vicar Carpegna sent out a series of notices. Some told parish priests to clean their churches and provide hangings for the sacristy. Others were addressed to women of ill-repute, asking them to avoid public scandal. Hoteliers were told not to raise their prices and artisans and shopkeepers were advised to respect feast days.

The religious ceremonies were particularly splendid, attracting large numbers of pilgrims. Artists prepared the basilicas for these ceremonies, often modifying them completely inside. One of these "theatres", as they were commonly called, was specially set up for the canonisation of Gaetano da Thiene, Ludovico Bertan, Filippo Benizi and Rosa da Lima, the first Latin American saint. Art glorified the 1675 Jubilee. Bernini was preparing a tabernacle for the Chapel of the Blessed Sacrament in St.Peter's and architects Carlo Fontana and Francesco Borromini were also working at that time in Rome.

| 1300 |
| 1350 |
| 1390 |
| 1400 |
| 1423 |
| 1450 |
| 1475 |
| 1500 |
| 1525 |
| 1550 |
| 1575 |
| 1600 |
| 1625 |
| 1650 |
| **1675** | 15th jubilee |
| 1700 |
| 1725 |
| 1750 |
| 1775 |
| 1825 |
| 1875 |
| 1900 |
| 1925 |
| 1950 |
| 1975 |
| 2000 |

# INNOCENT XII
# CLEMENT XI

Two popes
were involved
in the Holy Year of
1700: Innocent XII and Clement XI. Innocent, born An-
tonio Pignatelli, proclaimed the Jubilee but was unable to
attend the opening ceremony because of his feeble
health, and had to be substituted by a cardinal. In spite of
his great age (he was eighty-six at the beginning of his
pontificate in 1691) and his poor health, Innocent made
frequent visits to the Jubilee basilicas, to the amazement
of watching pilgrims. Later in the Holy Year, the Pope's
illness forced him to reduce the number of his visits, and
then he died on September 27, 1700. During the two
months of vacancy before a new pope was elected, few
pilgrims travelled to Rome.
The Holy Year of 1700 was memorable for its strongly
devotional quality. Pope Innocent gave it a particularly
spiritual imprint, and more attention was paid to the condition required for indulgences: a state of grace, to be
achieved through the sacrament of penance. It was with

1691-1700
1700-1721

this in mind that the Grand Penitentiary, Card.Colleredo, would go every day to St.Peter's to hear confessions and other cardinals and prelates did likewise, to help pilgrims with their confessions. Assistance to pil-

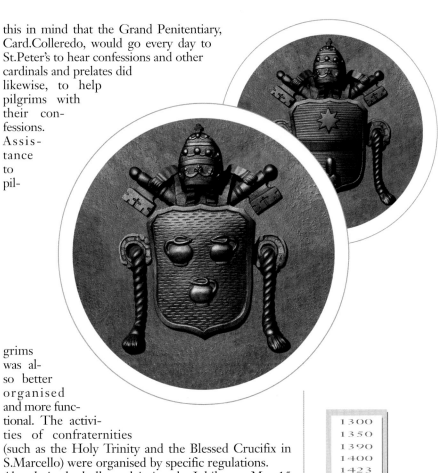

grims was also better organised and more functional. The activities of confraternities (such as the Holy Trinity and the Blessed Crucifix in S.Marcello) were organised by specific regulations. Already in the bull proclaiming the Jubilee on May 15 1699, Pope Innocent had given this calm, serene orientation to the Holy Year. The bull was called "*Regi seculorum...*". It was full of biblical allusions and quotations, and urged the faithful to come to Rome as a symbol of man's pilgrimage to the city of God. This Pope's qualities of gentleness and humility were particularly evident when he tried to bring peace between France and Germany during the reign of Louis XIV. He abolished papal nepotism and used all of St.Peter's financial resources to help the poor, who adored him, "Veni, pater pauperum".

Clement XI succeeded Innocent XII after a two-month conclave. It was late November, and an uneventful Holy Year was drawing to a close, when the Tiber river overflowed. Pilgrims could no longer reach St.Paul's, so they made their visits to S.Maria in Trastevere instead. The Holy Year solemnly ended on Christmas Day, 1700.

| |
|---|
| 1300 |
| 1350 |
| 1390 |
| 1400 |
| 1423 |
| 1450 |
| 1475 |
| 1500 |
| 1525 |
| 1550 |
| 1575 |
| 1600 |
| 1625 |
| 1650 |
| 1675 |
| **1700**    16th jubilee |
| 1725 |
| 1750 |
| 1775 |
| 1825 |
| 1875 |
| 1900 |
| 1925 |
| 1950 |
| 1975 |
| 2000 |

# BENEDICT XIII

It is said
that when the
Dominican friar
Vincenzo Maria Orsini
was elected pope, he asked for
his superior's permission before accepting, though at the
time he was Archbishop of Benevento. In any case, he
certainly kept a Dominican spirit throughout his pontificate, and often went back to visit the monastery where
he had lived as a simple friar. His behaviour was always
upright and saintly. He was severe with himself and with
others, and was always concerned with the pastoral side
of his role, just as he had been when he was a bishop. He
visited the sick and people in jail, helped the poor and
practised both material and spiritual charity. It was in
this spirit that he proclaimed a Jubilee on June 26, 1724,
with the bull "*Redemptor et Dominus noster*". Less than a
month had passed since his election. In the bull, Benedict urged the faithful to celebrate the Holy Year without ostentation, through prayer and repentance. Later

1724-1730

on, he fixed the conditions for obtaining indulgences required from anyone who could not physically come to Rome, meaning cloistered orders, the sick and people in prisons.

In another brief dated April 1725, Benedict XIII made a concession: Holy Year indulgences could be applied to the souls of dead people "per modum suffragii". Contemporary accounts tell us that this Jubilee had a profoundly spiritual quality, noticeable both in the religious ceremonies and in processions organised by the confraternities. The Pope insisted on austerity, forbidding the traditional illuminations and parades. He also forbid every kind of worldly amusement that year, including Carnival, costumes, parties and even playing the lottery. Benedict was himself the most devoted of pilgrims: he visited the Jubilee basilicas and spent a day with prisoners in the Capitoline jail; he even washed the feet of poor people. He personally listened to confessions in St.Peter's, taking the role of Grand Penitentiary. And he tried to keep down the price of food in Rome, which usually soared during Holy Years. A new event occurred that year: a synod for bishops of the Roman provinces was held in St.John Lateran, which established norms for the religious and ecclesiastic life. And decisions were made on other topics: for example, the synod set the guidelines on teaching catechism. Maria Clementina Stuart, granddaughter of John Sobieski and wife of James Stuart, was one of this Holy Year's pilgrims. She stayed on in Rome afterwards, and when she died in 1735 she was buried in St.Peter's. During that year, a son was born to Maria Clementina and her husband. Later on, he was ordained a priest, became a cardinal, then Archpriest of St.Peter's and Bishop of Frascati. The ruler of Siena, Violante Beatrice of Bavaria was also among the pilgrims that year. And three hundred and seventy slaves came to Rome after being liberated in Tunis. The 100,000 scudi paid to free them had been donated by the Confraternity of the Holy Trinity. This event fittingly crowned a memorable Jubilee.

| |
|---|
| 1300 |
| 1350 |
| 1390 |
| 1400 |
| 1423 |
| 1450 |
| 1475 |
| 1500 |
| 1525 |
| 1550 |
| 1575 |
| 1600 |
| 1625 |
| 1650 |
| 1675 |
| 1700 |
| **1725** — 17th jubilee |
| 1750 |
| 1775 |
| 1825 |
| 1875 |
| 1900 |
| 1925 |
| 1950 |
| 1975 |
| 2000 |

# BENEDICT XIV

In 1750, when Benedict XIV (Prospero Lambertini) had already been pope for ten years, he celebrated the mid-century Holy Year. He had already prepared the faithful for this event in several official documents which showed his gifts as a jurist and pastor. These documents gave all the requirements for celebrating the Jubilee, establishing the sacrament of confession as the fundamental requisite for obtaining indulgence.

1740-1758

The first of these documents was an encyclical, *"Annus qui"*, dated February 19, 1749. It addressed all the bishops in the Papal States on the topic of "church rites and cleanliness, ceremonies and religious music". Its goal was to ensure that every aspect of the Church within Rome and inside the Papal States would be ready and in perfect order for the Holy Year. Piety was to be encouraged, showiness of any kind was banned; while the liturgy and singing of sacred music were to achieve a higher standard. The bull proclaiming the Jubilee ("*Peregrinantes a Domino*", May 5, 1749) was actually an invitation to all mankind, not just Catholics but also heretics and schismatic. Everyone was invited to come to Rome and achieve salvation.

In a letter sent out to all the bishops on June 26 1749, the Pope knowledgeably discussed the biblical, liturgical and canonical origins of the Holy Year. A pilgrimage to Rome was not enough to reap its rewards; the sacraments of confession and communion were also necessary. With this in mind, Benedict sent letters to all the confessors in Rome, instructing them on their role.

Through all these documents, Benedict gave a definitive form to the Holy Year celebrations. The pope was to send a personal announcement of the Jubilee to every head of state, reminding them that the occasion should provide a stimulus to purify their conduct and moral standards. Without confession and repentance, no-one could receive forgiveness.

The Pope organised catechism sessions and spiritual exercises for the people of Rome in fourteen churches. One of the religious men chosen to instruct the Roman populace was friar, Leonardo da Porto Maurizio. He was so popular that huge crowds gathered to hear him preach in Piazza Navona on various occasions. They also squeezed into S.Maria in Trastevere and S.Maria sopra Minerva to listen to fra Leonardo, and were led by him along the stations of the Cross, around the Colosseum.

Great numbers of pilgrims came to Rome, and Pope Benedict was an example of faith and piety to them all. He visited the premises of confraternities as well as the palaces they had rented for the occasion. And Benedict's frequent appearances in the basilicas gave a particularly impressive quality to every religious ceremony.

Pilgrims who came to Rome in 1750 were spiritually enriched by the Holy Year rituals and the Pope, who was pleased with the Jubilee's results, encouraged them to keep up this standard of devotion and renewel even after the Holy Year was over.

| |
|---|
| 1300 |
| 1350 |
| 1390 |
| 1400 |
| 1423 |
| 1450 |
| 1475 |
| 1500 |
| 1525 |
| 1550 |
| 1575 |
| 1600 |
| 1625 |
| 1650 |
| 1675 |
| 1700 |
| 1725 |
| **1750**   18th jubilee |
| 1775 |
| 1825 |
| 1875 |
| 1900 |
| 1925 |
| 1950 |
| 1975 |
| 2000 |

# CLEMENT XIV
# PIUS VI

Two po-
pes put in
their efforts for the
nineteenth Holy Year: Clement XIV and Pius VI.
Pope Clement (born Lorenzo Ganganelli, a Franciscan)
published the bull for the 1775 Jubilee, "*Salutis nostrae*",
on April 30, 1774. But he died on the following September 22, and did not therefore inaugurate the Holy Year. It
could have given him the spiritual joy he needed, after the
many bitter events of his short pontificate. A particular
source of bitterness to Clement was the suppression of the
Society of Jesus on July 23, 1773.

The Society's abolition had been brought about by the
kings of the most important nations, whose Catholic heritage should have kept them from insisting on this step,
which damaged the Catholic church and was a source of
grief to the Pope. In the bull, Clement showed that he was
a true father of the poor, a man who loved peace and tried
unsuccessfully to convert his fellow man to this love of
peace.

1769-1774
1775-1799

The conclave after Clement's death lasted one hundred and thirty-seven days. Finally, Cardinal Gianangelo Braschi was elected on February 15, 1775, and he took the name of Pius VI. The traditional Holy Year inauguration date had already lapsed

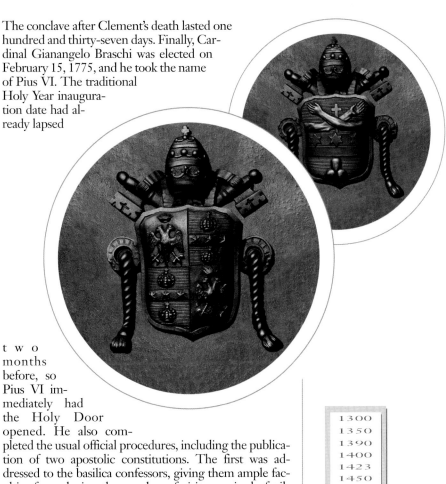

t w o months before, so Pius VI immediately had the Holy Door opened. He also completed the usual official procedures, including the publication of two apostolic constitutions. The first was addressed to the basilica confessors, giving them ample faculties for reducing the number of visits required of pilgrims, in exchange for other acts of piety. This applied especially to the sick, to people in prisons and to the cloistered orders. The Pope also published Clement XIV's bull, "*Salutis nostrae auctor*", in Italian.

The 1775 Holy Year worked out better than could have been hoped at the time of Clement XIV's death.

Considering the epoch in which it took place, a great number of pilgrims came to Rome that year. Anna Maria Taigi was one of the pilgrims, and she never left Rome afterwards.

It was the last Jubilee of the eighteenth century. The currents of revolutionary thought which were about to be unleashed on the other side of the Alps, was also to sweep like a hurricane through Italy. Rome was occupied by the French troops in 1797. Pius VI was torn away from his city and banished to Valence, in France, where he died in 1799.

| |
|---|
| 1300 |
| 1350 |
| 1390 |
| 1400 |
| 1423 |
| 1450 |
| 1475 |
| 1500 |
| 1525 |
| 1550 |
| 1575 |
| 1600 |
| 1625 |
| 1650 |
| 1675 |
| 1700 |
| 1725 |
| 1750 |
| **1775** — 19th jubilee |
| 1825 |
| 1875 |
| 1900 |
| 1925 |
| 1950 |
| 1975 |
| 2000 |

# LEO XII

The 1800 Jubilee was never celebrated.

After the death of Pius VI in France on August 29, 1799, it took three months to decide where the next conclave would be held; finally, Venice was chosen. Pius VII was elected on March 14, 1800, but he did not reach Rome until July. The climate of uncertainty, of political changes and war, made the celebration unadvisable.

The next Holy Year took place in 1825, starting out in an atmosphere of fear and mistrust. When Pope Leo XII (Annibale della Genga) expressed his intention of celebrating the Holy Year, many cardinals, princes and ambassadors were against him.

The general fear was that revolutionaries might mingle with the pilgrims, instigating the population to revolt and provoking a carnage.

People still remembered the 1821 rebellion. But the Pope, who was optimistic and resolute man, proclaimed

1823-1829

the next jubilee on May 24, 1824 with the bull *"Quod hoc inuente saeculo"*, inviting the faithful to come "to this holy Jerusalem, the city which, because of Peter's faith, now reigns over the world". The Pope gave instructions on how to earn the Jubilee indulgence and on visiting the patriarchal basilicas.

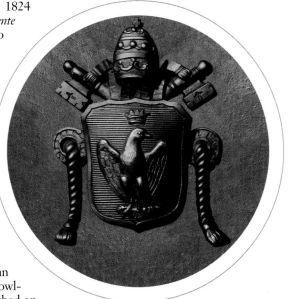

St.Paul's Outside the Walls was no longer on the list of these basilicas: it had been destroyed by fire in July, 1823. S.Maria in Trastevere was to be visited instead.

There were less pilgrims than usual that year. Leo XII acknowledged this fact in a bull published on December 23, 1825, when just a few days before the Holy Year was over, he extended it for another six months. He also noted that "neither in this city, or in any of the countries through which the pilgrims travelled, was there any turbulence or disorder". Some of pilgrims were rather unusual, such as the Austrian army regiments, who were leaving the Kingdom of Naples after the 1821 rebellion. They were granted a special jubilee indulgence, after receiving confession and holy communion, and after each corps had visited St.Peter's just once. Other pilgrims included the magistrate of Rome and all the members of the Capitoline government. The jubilee indulgence received by the bandit Gasparone and all his gang was also a memorable event. Massimo D'Azelio found these episodes annoying, and declared that he could not bear to see Rome "transformed for twelve months into a vast society of spiritual exercises".

Future saints such as Vincent Pallotti, Gaspare del Bufalo and Anna Maria Taigi, were all living in Rome at that time, and so were the Blessed Elisabetta Canori Mora and the Venerable Maria Cristina of Savoy.

This Holy Year also held a personally enriching experience for Gioacchino Belli, who was just a young boy at the time. Shortly after the Holy Door was opened, Belli recited a composition in Latin written for the occasion. It was in the Cortile del Belvedere, where the Pope was receiving his guests. To thank him, Belli was given a silver medal of the Jubilee.

| |
|---|
| 1300 |
| 1350 |
| 1390 |
| 1400 |
| 1423 |
| 1450 |
| 1475 |
| 1500 |
| 1525 |
| 1550 |
| 1575 |
| 1600 |
| 1625 |
| 1650 |
| 1675 |
| 1700 |
| 1725 |
| 1750 |
| 1775 |
| **1825** — 20th jubilee |
| 1875 |
| 1900 |
| 1925 |
| 1950 |
| 1975 |
| 2000 |

# PIUS IX

This Pope could have celebrated two jubilees during the twenty-nine years of his pontificate, in 1850 and in 1875. However, he was not able to proclaim either one of these Holy Years. Owing to an extremely difficult political situation, Pius had to leave Rome on November 24, 1848 and retreat to Gaeta, in the Kingdom of Naples. This event made it impossible to celebrate the Jubilee in the usual way. Pius IX only granted an indulgence "as a form of Jubilee" during the novena for the feast of St.Peter and St.Paul. It was a kind of "supplementary" jubilee, which produced good results, as the Pope himself noted with pleasure in the encyclical *"Exultavit cor nostrum"* published on November 21, 1851.

The 1875 Jubilee, on the other hand, was officially considered the twenty-first Holy Year of the series, even though the traditional events of a jubilee did not

1846-1878

take place: times were hard. Pius IX discussed this in a bull, *"Gravibus ecclesiae et huius saeculi calamitatibus"*, of December 24, 1874. "The serious causes which impeded our celebration of the 1850 Jubilee, instead of having subsided, are increasing daily, according to God's will". In spite of the variety of evils then befalling the Church, Pius IX announced that all of 1875 was to be a universal and great jubilee. This was proof of the Pope's great faith and courage. Courage in facing a difficult situation after Rome was seized in 1870. And faith, because in spite of the fact that he was virtually held prisoner in the Vatican, Pius showed that he was in full possession of his spiritual power, and used this power to its utmost to help the world's faithful.

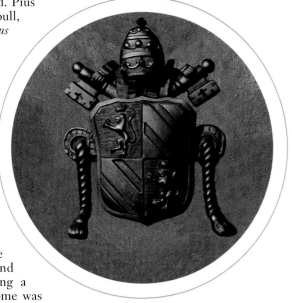

Circumstances inevitably limited the usual exterior manifestations of the Jubilee: neither the opening of the Holy Door or ceremonial pilgrimages took place. The extraordinary aspect of this Jubilee was that the Pope did not circumscribe the indulgence to Rome, but extended it to the whole world.

Pilgrimages did however take place: people came from France, Belgium, the United States, Mexico and Germany. They came to receive the Jubilee indulgence, but they also wanted to express their solidarity with the imprisoned Pope. A group of pilgrims came from Bologna, composed of members of the newly-formed "Azione Cattolica" movement. Since they arrived in Rome during January, 1876, Pius extended the Holy Year for these young men's benefit. The Pope himself earned a Jubilee indulgence by entering St.Peter's on February 11, when the doors of the Basilica were closed.

| |
|---|
| 1300 |
| 1350 |
| 1390 |
| 1400 |
| 1423 |
| 1450 |
| 1475 |
| 1500 |
| 1525 |
| 1550 |
| 1575 |
| 1600 |
| 1625 |
| 1650 |
| 1675 |
| 1700 |
| 1725 |
| 1750 |
| 1775 |
| 1825 |
| **1875**    21ˢᵗ jubilee |
| 1900 |
| 1925 |
| 1950 |
| 1975 |
| 2000 |

# LEO XIII

When Leo XIII (Gioacchino Pecci) became pope, the Church no longer had temporal supremacy: Rome was *"sub hostii dominatione constituta"*. In spite of this, Leo XIII attitude towards the new Italy was essentially benevolent. His relations with foreign governments and kingdoms were usually good, and his abilities lent increasing prestige to the Church.

1878-1903

These abilities were evident when he settled the conflict between the Caroline Islands and Spain. Everyone appreciated his intelligence and knowledge of humanistic and philosophical topics, which facilitated his success in diplomacy.

Leo encouraged religious training, stimulating the clergy's spiritual and cultural growth, and reunited dissident factions; he supported missionaries and tried to resolve social issues.

The Pope's encyclicals provided both enlightenment and possible solutions to problems.

In time, respect and admiration for the Pope turned into love.

This was noticeable in the demostrations of heartfelt affection he received on various occasions, such as the fiftieth anniversary of his ordination (1887), his fifty years as a bishop (1896), the sixtieth anniversary of his priesthood (1898) and his ninetieth birthday (1900).

Leo proclaimed the Holy Year of 1900 on May 11, 1899, with the bull *"Properante ad exitum"*. This document contains charming memories of the Pope's past, but he also sadly denounces the evils of his time. But the new century was dedicated to Christ and his redeeming power.

The Holy Door was opened by Leo XIII in an atmosphere of great enthusiasm: the faithful cheered the old Pope, who looked tired but radiant. Lorenzo Perosi directed Palestrina's "Iubilate Deo", last sung in 1825. Then the pilgrims arrived. Although some people considered the opening of the Holy Door as a kind of provocation, the Italian government tried in every way to respect the promises made when Rome became the capital city of Italy. Unfortunately, not everyone understood this, and the more bitter anticlerical factions protested. The Masons actually proclaimed their own jubilee on September 20, including visits "to the four lay basilicas": the Pantheon, the Janiculum, Porta Pia and the Capitoline hill.

Giovanni Pascoli dedicated a poem to Leo called "The Holy Door", which has been described as "the most dazzling poem" about the Jubilee; it is certainly one of the most inspired documents of the Holy Year of 1900.

Crosses were put on the highest mountains of Italy, tangible signs of dedication to Christ the Redeemer. Leo XIII then closed the Holy Door, and in a "Carmen saeculare" he composed, wished peace on mankind and all the nations.

| |
|---|
| 1300 |
| 1350 |
| 1390 |
| 1400 |
| 1423 |
| 1450 |
| 1475 |
| 1500 |
| 1525 |
| 1550 |
| 1575 |
| 1600 |
| 1625 |
| 1650 |
| 1675 |
| 1700 |
| 1725 |
| 1750 |
| 1775 |
| 1825 |
| 1875 |
| **1900** — 22nd jubilee |
| 1925 |
| 1950 |
| 1975 |
| 2000 |

# PIUS XI

Born in De-
sio in 1857, the
future pope studied
in the seminaries of Mi-
lan and Rome. He was a scholar,
and first worked in libraries, both in Italy and abroad.
When Pius X nominated him prefect of the Vatican Library, he was already working in a similar capacity at the
Ambrosian Library in Milan. After an appointment as
apostolic nunzio to Poland, he was nominated archbishop
of Milan. In 1922 he was elected pope, taking the name of
Pius XI. The new Pope's decision to give his first "Urbi et
Orbi" blessing from the external loggia of St.Peter's
caused considerable surprise. This loggia on the façade of
the church opens onto the square of St.Peter's, and had
been closed since the breach in the walls of Porta Pia in
1870. Pius XI's gesture was an indication that something
was changing. And Pius did close the "Roman issue" in
1929, with the Lateran Treaty. This gesture was an indication of Pius XI's firm character and the clarity of vision

1922-1939

he intended to use in guiding the Church, bringing it into the modern era.

He encouraged missionary activities and opened new paths for the Azione Cattolica movement.

On December 23, 1922 Pius XI announced that there would be a Jubilee, but it was officially proclaimed, on May 29, 1924. In the inaugural bull, *"Infinita Dei misericordia"*, the Pope focused on the Jubilee's extraordinary significance: it had the power to sanctify every individual Catholic, and to unite in brotherhood all the faithful visiting Rome. Pius XI opened the Holy Door in St.Peter's on December 24, 1924.

Bishops stood by to hand him the hammer and chisel used to break down the wall, a sign of their communion with the Pope and a symbol of their desire to pass on to the faithful the spiritual riches which the Pope alone possesses. There were about 600,000 pilgrims, and for the first time a central committee guided and assisted them. Several canonisations occurred that year: eight Jesuit martyrs from Canada, seventy-nine martyrs from Corea, 32 martyrs from Orange; and Teresa of Lisieux. Since the Pope wanted to give a strongly missionary imprint to this Holy Year, he ordered that an exhibition on this theme be set up in the Vatican Palace and gardens. This spirit influenced even place names in Vatican City: to this day, there is a square inside its walls called Largo della Capanna Cinese, taking its name from a Chinese hut.

Pilgrims who visited Rome were able to experience the Church's universality, seeing its openness to every country and getting an idea of the work done by missionaries to spread Christ's message through religious channels, but also through charitable and social activities. On December 23, 1925, shortly before the Holy Year was due to close, the Pope established the feast of Christ the King, a reminder of this jubilee.

It was a feast that glorified the spirit of "unitas gentium" achieved during the Holy Year. In celebrating Christ as Word Incarnate and Redeemer, the Church fulfils its mission of drawing mankind towards Christ, who is the saviour of us all.

| |
|---|
| 1300 |
| 1350 |
| 1390 |
| 1400 |
| 1423 |
| 1450 |
| 1475 |
| 1500 |
| 1525 |
| 1550 |
| 1575 |
| 1600 |
| 1625 |
| 1650 |
| 1675 |
| 1700 |
| 1725 |
| 1750 |
| 1775 |
| 1825 |
| 1875 |
| 1900 |
| **1925** — 23rd jubilee |
| 1950 |
| 1975 |
| 2000 |

## The 1929 Jubilee

Following the example set by Leo XIII, who had celebrated the fiftieth anniversary of his priestly ordination, Pius proclaimed a universal jubilee for his own fiftieth year of priesthood. Originally the Jubilee was meant only for Rome (Apostolic Constitution *"Auspicantibus nobis"* of January 6, 1929). But towards the end of 1929 it was extended to the whole world until the end of 1930 (Encyclical *"Quinquagesimo ante anno"*, December 23, 1929). This "extraordinary" jubilee was a formal affair. Its most interesting and joyful pilgrims were seminarians, who came to Rome from all over the world.

## The 1933 Jubilee (photograph)

Pius XI proclaimed another extraordinary jubilee, which he called the Redemption Jubilee. He announced it to the cardinals as they gathered around him on Christmas Eve, 1932. He told them: of all the extraordinary jubilees, this will be the most remarkable one of all. It was to be a devout and grateful commemoration of the Redemption, which had worked miracles, changed the world and begun a new era for humanity: *"Novus saeculorum nascitur ordo"*. The bull *"Quod nuper"*, published on January 6, 1933, defined this Holy Year's time span, from April 2, 1933 (Passion Sunday) to April 2, 1934 (Easter Monday).

It also touched on Christ's universal regality, reproposed to humanity with the theme of redemption. Many pilgrims came to Rome that year, particularly for special events which had a personal meaning to specific groups of people, such as the canonisations of Bernadette Soubirous, St.Louise de Marillac and St.John Bosco. According to contemporary accounts, 300,000 people took part in the canonisation ceremony for St.John Bosco, and the Pope blessed them from the external loggia of St.Peter's. One thing was clear: the Church was offering salvation to the world, not just individually but universally. And many people were attracted, responding positively to its call.

# PIUS XII

The image
of Pius XII is
still in our mind's
eye, slender and impos-
ing, a tall and solemn figure.

1939-1958

His bearing and gestures were hieratic; so was the way
he held his arms when praying, the way he knelt and
the way he preached. When he blessed the faithful, the
Pope would open his arms and become a living cross.
His angelic appearance and loveable personal traits
made his extraordinary intelligence and profound
goodness all the more admirable. He enjoyed being
with people. Even before the Holy Year, his audiences
attracted pilgrims from all over the world. And Pius
talked to them about their problems and aspirations,
speaking in several languages.
He used encyclicals and various types of messages to
teach mankind the principles of social justice, which
along with charity, produce true peace. He firmly and
gently guided humanity towards achieving this peace.

He had warned, "Nothing is lost through peace. Everything can be lost through war"; but no-one listened to him and war destroyed everything. Only the Pope's charity remained, and he extended it to everyone: the victims of bombardments, prisoners in concentration camps, the defenceless, persecuted Jews. They called him "Defensor civitatis".

The war was over, and the survivors were making their way home. On the feast of the Ascension, on May 26, 1949, Pius XII proclaimed the Holy Year with the bull *Iubilaeum maximum*. It was an invitation to forgiveness, to brotherhood and to world peace. Already by Christmas 1948 the entire Catholic world was praying for the Holy Year. The prayer had been composed by the Pope himself. It called down God's blessing on the "year of the great return and great forgiveness". Pius discussed this description of the Holy Year in a message he imparted to all the world on December 23, 1949, the day before the Holy Door was opened. He also discussed the evils oppressing mankind, inviting everyone to come to Rome, which would welcome them with loving arms.

The Holy Door was opened on December 24. At the end of the ceremony, the Pope went to the Chapel of the Blessed Sacrament, where he blessed the new bronze panels for the evening closure of the Holy Door. These new doors substituted the wooden doors which Benedict XIV had inaugurated on December 24, 1749. The new panels made by sculptor Vico Consorti "movingly praise the wonders of mercy practised by God, who came to look for what had been lost" (Pius XII).

Three and a half million people came to Rome for the 1950 Holy Year. The reason for this success lies partly in the fact that people still listened to the Church's admonitions. A strong clash between Catholicism and the Marxists world was also felt acutely in those years, and participating in the Jubilee gave Catholics a way of choosing sides. Pius XII's own power to attract pil-

| |
|---|
| 1300 |
| 1350 |
| 1390 |
| 1400 |
| 1423 |
| 1450 |
| 1475 |
| 1500 |
| 1525 |
| 1550 |
| 1575 |
| 1600 |
| 1625 |
| 1650 |
| 1675 |
| 1700 |
| 1725 |
| 1750 |
| 1775 |
| 1825 |
| 1875 |
| 1900 |
| 1925 |
| **1950** 24th jubilee |
| 1975 |
| 2000 |

grims should also not be underestimated. The Church offered pilgrims a jubilee, by means of a Pope whose luminous presence throughout their stay in Rome was to be one of their dearest memories of the Holy Year.

On December 23, 1950, when the Jubilee was about to end, Pius XII discussed the results of that year, "which - he said - has left a mark so deep in the life of the Church that even the most optimistic expectations have been surpassed".

Extraordinary events had occurred, such as the canonisation of two very young saints, Domenico Savio and Maria Goretti.

During Maria Goretti's glorification, attended by the Saint's mother, Rome was taken over by the young women's faction of the Azione Cattolica movement.

The definition of the dogma of Mary's bodily Assumption to heaven, which was proclaimed in St.Peter's on November 1, 1950 was a high point of this Holy Year.

It was a glorious day, even weather-wise. That morning the sunlight was particularly bright, and the moon could still be seen in the sky.

The heavens themselves seemed to be exhaulting Mary, in the words of the liturgy, "Pulchra ut luna, electa ut sol". This ferment continued, one might say, until the end of Pius XII's pontificate in 1958. And the Pope, who had been the protagonist of that Holy Year, continued to attract people and radiate light.

# PAUL VI

On May 9,
1973, Paul VI
announced     the
new jubilee during a
papal audience in St.Peter's:
"We want to give you a piece of information which we
consider important for the Church - he said - and it is
this. After having prayed and thought, we have decided
to celebrate the next Holy Year in 1975, after twenty-five
years, according to the guidelines established by our predecessor Paul II...". This announcement was unexpected and caused some surprise, also because it was made so
much before the beginning of Holy Year. It was however a timely answer to protests against the Holy Year tradition, which considered the jubilee unsuitable to modern times. These protesters felt no interest in the rituals
of past centuries and supported the religious lifestyle
proposed by Vatican II.
The Pope's decision, reached after much reflection and
prayer, was discussed in its practical aspects during many

1963-1978

general audiences: contemporary man had to be helped to achieve that inner renewal proposed by Vatican II. And the jubilee renewal itself could only be accomplished through reconciliation on a vast scale, within the religious community, society, politics and ecumenism.

During his speech on May 9, 1973, Paul VI also disclosed an important aspect of the forthcoming Holy Year. The Jubilee celebrations were still to take place in Rome, but they would be preceded by celebrations in local churches. Everyone would thus be given a chance for renewal and reconciliation, preparing for the conclusive moment of the Jubilee, in front of the tombs of the apostles in Rome. This innovation also had the intent of honouring local churches, where celebrations would begin on Pentecost, June 10, 1973.

The announcement was followed on the feast of the Ascension (May 23, 1974) by the bull proclaiming the Jubilee, "*Apostolorum limina*". The bull was very rich in content. After a good synthesis of the origins and nature of the Holy Year, the Pope outlined this one's goal: achieving renewal and reconciliation in both individuals and the entire Church. This would be a concrete response to modern man's aspirations to freedom, justice, unity and peace.

The Jubilee celebrations began on December 24, 1974, on Christmas night. The whole context of the celebration had changed: the liturgical renewal of Vatican II inevitably had its effect. Moreover, the ceremony was not just seen by the faithful present in St.Peter's, but by almost one billion people around the world via a special television link activated by 45 different channels. The ceremony started out in the entrance to the basilica. After opening the Holy Door, the Pope knelt on the threshold to pray, then entered the church and celebrated midnight Mass. During the homily, Paul VI invited all the faithful to celebrate Christ's Nativity together, and together achieve the jubilee of renewal and reconciliation.

The Pope's request to God to achieve this union was en-

| | |
|---|---|
| 1300 | |
| 1350 | |
| 1390 | |
| 1400 | |
| 1423 | |
| 1450 | |
| 1475 | |
| 1500 | |
| 1525 | |
| 1550 | |
| 1575 | |
| 1600 | |
| 1625 | |
| 1650 | |
| 1675 | |
| 1700 | |
| 1725 | |
| 1750 | |
| 1775 | |
| 1825 | |
| 1875 | |
| 1900 | |
| 1925 | |
| 1950 | |
| 1975 | 25th jubilee |
| 2000 | |

dorsed by a special penance he practised that evening: he was wearing a hairshirt. This Holy Year, according to what Paul VI told the cardinals in a speech held on December 22, shortly before the Jubilee ended, was intentionally low-key, without outer display. It was a purely religious event, where the meaning of prayer was rediscovered. It was an event of the people: for the most important pilgrimages were made by humble, simple people from all over the world, including third-world countries, who gave splendid proof of their faith in the Church. It was an orderly event: in spite of the great tide of pilgrims flowing into Rome, everything was well organised and the great celebrations took place without mishaps. Moments of grace and inspiration were experienced during thirteen beatifications and six canonisations, confirming the Church's universal vocation to sanctity, which Vatican II had already recognised. The Holy Year ended on Christmas night in St.Peter's square.

The ceremony was broadcast on television and on the radio in most of the world and was watched by hundreds of millions of people; its heterogeneous quality was aptly represented by the crowds who had gathered in St.Peter's square. The ceremony had three distinct phases: the initial "statio" in St.Peter's, with the clergy aligned in a procession in the nave; pausing in the entrance, where the Pope closed the Holy Door, saying the doxological formula, and the answering Amen of the faithful. The third phase started when the 'Gloria in excelsis Deo' was intoned and the formal ceremo-

ny of Christmas Mass began. This was the first time that it was celebrated in St.Peter's square, which is the most beautiful square in the world. Paul VI's homily marked the passage between the Holy Year and resuming the journey towards Christ the Lord.

# JOHN PAUL II

Pope John Paul II first announced that an extraordinary jubilee would be held in 1983 during a speech to the College of Cardinals on November 26, 1982. Since 1983 was the 1,950th anniversary of the Redemption, the Pope decided to dedicate an entire year to commemorating this mystery, so that it could sink more deeply into the thoughts and actions of the entire Church.

The Jubilee was proclaimed on January 6, 1983, with the bull *"Aperite portas Redemptori"*. The bull's title was a reminder of the appeal which John Paul had made shortly after being elected pope. On October 22, 1978, when he began his apostolic ministry, John Paul II had cried out to the whole world from St.Peter's square, "Open the doors to Christ...". The bull also contained the dates for beginning and ending the Jubilee. It was to begin on March 25, the feast of the An-

1978

nunciation. And it was to end on April 22, 1984, which was Easter Sunday, "the day when joy overflows because of Christ's redeeming sacrifice, which perpetually renews and nourishes the Church". Several passages of the bull listed the conditions for acquiring the jubilee indulgence: confession and communion, and taking part in a liturgical ceremony within ones diocese or parish: a Mass, a celebration of the Word, a penitential ceremony, a consecration of the sacraments or following the stations of the Cross. The places where indulgences could be acquired were also listed. In Rome these included the four patriarchal basilicas, the catacombs and the church of S.Croce in Gerusalemme. Outside the city, bishops had the right to decide which religious places within their diocese could receive pilgrimages.

The Jubilee would be celebrated at the same time throughout the world as the "Year of the Lord's Grace" for the entire Church.

The Holy Door in St.Peter's was opened by John Paul II. A penitential procession accompanied him from the church of S.Stefano degli Abissini to the entrance of St.Peter's.

The Pope then opened the door, swinging it on its hinges. After kneeling at length in prayer on the threshold, the Pope entered the basilica and said Mass. On that same day, it was officially made known that Umberto di Savoia (Italy's former king) had left the Pope the relic of the Holy Shroud in his will. This relic, which is kept in Turin, bears eloquent witness to the Redemption.

This extraordinary Holy Year ended on Easter, 1984. John Paul II discussed its spiritual effects in a homily, where he touched on the sharing of spiritual riches among the thousands of pilgrims who came to Rome for the occasion. Looking towards the post-jubilee period, the Pope emphasised the urgent need for modern man to open his doors to Christ the Redeemer. The motivation given for the Holy Year in the indic-

| |
|---|
| 1300 |
| 1350 |
| 1390 |
| 1400 |
| 1423 |
| 1450 |
| 1475 |
| 1500 |
| 1525 |
| 1550 |
| 1575 |
| 1600 |
| 1625 |
| 1650 |
| 1675 |
| 1700 |
| 1725 |
| 1750 |
| 1775 |
| 1825 |
| 1875 |
| 1900 |
| 1925 |
| 1950 |
| 1975 |
| 2000 |

tion bull was to become a guideline for all the faithful, the Pope said. And he concluded, "Let us open to Christ the doors of our complex modern world, of our society of increasing contrasts; let us give Christ the possibility of grafting the Redemption and a culture of love onto our world".

When the Mass was over, the Pope entered St.Peter's and said a prayer full of nostalgia for what was ending and faith in what would never end: "...We see the Holy Door of this temple close, but we know that the doors of your mercy will never be closed, O Father, to those who believe in your love and proclaim your mercy...".

The Pope, after having knelt on the threshold of the Holy Door and prayed in silence, closed the door's bronze panels, reciting the doxological formula, "Christ yesterday and today, beginning and end; he opens and no-one may close; he closes, and no-one may open. His is the power and the glory for ever and ever".

From 1983 onwards, the Redemption Jubilee has kept hope alive in everyone who worships the coming of the Lord and is getting ready to commemorate his physical presence on this earth in the year 2000.

# INDEX

# INDEX

# INDEX OF ILLUSTRATIONS

© Copyright 1999
Ats Italia Editrice
Via Francesco Sivori, 6 - 00136 Roma

ISBN 88-86542-69-0

*Author*
Virgilio Card. Noè

*Translation*
Iris Jones

*Editor*
Frida Giannini

*Graphics*
Sabrina Moroni (Ats Italia Editrice)

*Photolithography*
Scriba - Florence

*Printing*
Papergraf - Padova

*Photographs*
Photographic archives of the Fabbrica di S.Pietro (Photo G. Marcucci)
Ats Italia Editrice p. 104 (G. Galazka),
              pp.106-107 (C. Tini)

*Front cover photograph:* Vico Consorti, Holy Door, atrium of St.Peter's
*Back cover photograph:* St.Peter's façade